With objectives in mind

Guide to Science 5/13

Published for the Schools Council by
Macdonald Educational, London and New York

© Schools Council Publications 1972

First impression 1972
Second impression (with amendments) 1973
Third impression (with amendments) 1974
Fourth impression (with amendments) 1975
Fifth impression 1977

ISBN 0 356 04009 7

Published by
Macdonald Educational
Holywell House
Worship Street
London EC2A 2EN

850 Seventh Avenue
New York 10019

The chief authors of this book are:

Len Ennever	Project Director
Wynne Harlen	Evaluator

The other members of the Science 5/13 team are:

Albert James	Deputy Project Director

Sheila Parker
Don Radford
Roy Richards
Mary Horn

Made and printed by Waterlow (Dunstable) Limited

Preface

'Science 5/13' is a project sponsored jointly by the Schools Council, the Nuffield Foundation and the Scottish Education Department, and based at the University of Bristol School of Education. It aims at helping teachers to help children between the ages of five and thirteen years to learn science through first-hand experience using a variety of methods.

The Project has produced books, most of which comprise Units of work dealing with subject-areas in which children are likely to conduct investigations. These Units are linked by objectives that we hope children will attain through their work. This book, however, is different. In it we discuss the thinking that informs our way of working, and we show how we have arrived at the guide to *Objectives for children learning science*, printed at the back of the book.

Acknowledgements

Metrication

The Project is deeply grateful to its many friends: to the local education authorities who have helped us work in their areas, to those of their staff who, acting as area representatives, have borne the heavy brunt of administering our trials, and to the teachers, heads and wardens who have been generous without stint in working with their children on our materials. The books we have written drew substance from the work they did for us, and it was through their critical appraisal that our materials reached their present form. For guidance, we had our sponsors, our Consultative Committee and, for support in all our working, the University of Bristol. To all of them we acknowledge our many debts: their help has been invaluable.

This has given us a great deal to think about. We have been given much good advice by well-informed friends, and we have consulted many reports by learned bodies. Following the advice and the reports wherever possible we have expressed quantities in metric units with Imperial units afterwards in square brackets if it seemed useful to state them so.

There are, however, some cases to which the recommendations are difficult to apply. For instance we have difficulty with units such as miles per hour (which has statutory force in this country) and with some Imperial units that are still in current use for common commodities and, as far as we know, liable to remain so for some time. In these cases we have tried to use our common sense, and, in order to make statements that are both accurate and helpful to teachers we have quoted Imperial measures followed by the approximate metric equivalent in square brackets if it seemed sensible to give them.

Where we have quoted statements made by children, or given illustrations that are children's work, we have left unaltered the units in which the children worked—in any case some of these units were arbitrary.

Contents

Prologue

A classroom situation

You couldn't call it a quiet classroom, but you wouldn't call it a noisy one either. The teacher I had come to see was not in the room, but the class seemed unaware of his absence, and were working as I had often seen them work. They were ten-year-olds; a couple were reading, two or three were writing, a group of three or four were in a corner, arranging an exhibition of plastics, and one boy was sitting deep in thought, his elbows on the desk, his chin in his hands looking at the ceiling with his mouth pursed. The rest seemed gainfully employed in their various groups, and from the fact that there were a few empty places I gathered that some were working elsewhere. Most of the conversation came from a couple of groups occupied in activities of their own; one lot were kneeling on the floor round a small truck, pointing to it and debating; the other group were counting the swings of a pendulum hung from the lintel of the storeroom door; one of them had a stop-clock, another a paper clipped to a board; he was looking at it reflectively and was slowly scratching his head with a pencil.

As I watched, one of the boys from the floor group came over to the cupboard where I was standing. 'Can I help you, sir?' he asked.

'Is Mr Ford about?'

'No sir', he answered, 'He's down at the bottom of the field with the Tree Group. I don't suppose he'll be long, though. I'll tell him you're here, if you want me to.'

There were footsteps and voices in the corridor. The classroom door opened and Mr Ford came in, followed by three girls.

'Sorry I wasn't here when you came. Have you been waiting long?'

'No, only a moment. I came to return your photographs.'

'Thanks. I was out with a group working on trees. They've set themselves a fine problem: ''How do you estimate the number of leaves on a tree?'' '

'Have they got very far with it?'

'Oh yes. We think we've worked out a way of doing it, and they're just about ready to have a go. They've been discussing it among themselves all the week, on and off, so finally we decided to talk it over on the site; by the tree, that is. Most of them said it couldn't be done, but Phil Baker, who's not particularly bright but he does worry away at things, said, ''You could count the leaves on one branch and see how many branches there are.'' Of course they told him that all branches weren't the same, but Rachel said, ''If you stand back and look at this tree, you could judge how many times that branch would go into the whole area of the tree.''

'Well, there was an argument about that; then they decided it wasn't a bad idea, so now they're going to make what they call an ''area-judger''. It's a shoebox with a window cut out at one end, and a peep-hole at the other. You look through the peep-hole and move back till the patch of leaves you've counted just fills the window. Then, keeping the same distance from the tree, you go round it, still looking through the peep-hole, and count how many windows-full you get if you look at all the leaves and don't let your windows-full overlap. If you know the number of windows-full round the tree you ought to be able to work out how many leaves on the tree.'

'Aren't there a few snags to that, Mr Ford ?'

'Yes, there are. Some they'll see and some they won't, and there'll be arguments about whether it's fair or not, and what sort of estimate it is when you've got it, but that's all part of the game. And you never know whether someone else will come up with a completely different idea—we'll just have to see what happens. Anyway, when they've finished they won't be quite so ready to accept statements about how many and how much without asking "How do you know ?" '

'I suppose some of them get quite tough about that ?'

'Yes, indeed ; often they go through a period when they won't accept anything—the boys especially. And the arguments spread outside the group that starts them, often to the whole class if we have a class discussion on the subject.

'It's astonishing how much they know about what goes on in other groups. Look at those girls who came in with me. They're talking to the pendulum group. I'll bet they're discussing what they've been doing outside, and I wouldn't put it past one of the pendulum group to go back with them and have a look. Sometimes when they do that they stay for a bit, and may even join the other group temporarily if they've had an idea and want to work it out.

'A certain amount of swapping round like that does go on and I don't object, but I keep a sharp eye on it. We don't want too much of it, especially with some people.'

'It must take you all your time to keep track of what's going on.'

'Not really, you seem to develop a sixth sense about it after a time. Actually you learn to work in a way that keeps you informed.'

'It all looks a bit haphazard to me, but I suppose it's not.'

'Far from it. I have to know what's going on and what's liable to follow, because I have to make some provision ahead. But what I must know, in general terms, is what I want them to get out of what they're doing ; otherwise it would be haphazard.

'Of course, experience helps you there. You see, I've thought about it for years now, so I've got the general ideas clear at the back of my mind ; but I still have to do some pretty direct thinking about the value of particular activities to individual children. That's why I go round talking to them so much. And I find it helps me, and them as well, if they come and discuss with me any results they get from investigations as soon as they've got them and thought about them. It's a sort of class rule, and a very good one too for checking progress and planning ahead. They like doing it.'

'Does it go on like this all day ?'

'No, indeed ; they have a very varied time. Sometimes they do things all together, like dancing, swimming, games ; sometimes they split up for visits ; even when they're with me in the classroom they don't always work in the same way. Quite often we have class discussions about what we've been doing, perhaps with reports by individual children, or, if I've been doing a bit of straightforward class-teaching, as sometimes I do, there might be a discussion with part of the class. They might have become interested in something arising from what I've said, such as making a play about some incident or the other, and that gives rise to more group work. This present topic with the tree group was a case in point. Then, many of them will have an assignment of work on hand, and they will fit that into the pattern of group work.

'Most of the work they do gives rise to recording of some kind. They write accounts of what they've done, draw graphs of their results, make models; some of them even take photographs. Much of it goes on the classroom wall, as you can see; some of it they make into folders.'

A bell rang in the corridor.

'You still have bells.'

'Oh yes, a few. They mark important events in the day like dinner-time, when we mustn't be late.'

'Well it hasn't disturbed these people much.'

'No. They stay to school dinner but they're on second sitting, so most of them will go on with what they're doing. They get interested, and they like to finish if they can. They're not much given to clock-watching.'

I left them, and as I walked home I thought about the children, their teacher and the way they worked together. How different it was from twenty years ago. Habits of independent study were now firmly rooted, and children were accustomed to take the responsibility of work in groups or on their own. Some subject-areas had lent themselves well to this procedure, and in these the ways of working had been forged. Science had lagged behind a bit, perhaps because we had been slow to recognise a field of study that could rightly be called science at the primary level. We recognised it somewhat better now, but we still do not see clearly enough its relations with the structured science to which it joins later. It may be that those who work with children could best be helped by a study of what these children might achieve through work in science, and of how these achievements might be brought about. Such a study this Project has been commissioned to make.

1 The problem as we see it

Introduction

The most important of this Project's terms of reference is to help teachers help children to learn about science. From the beginning we thought it necessary to state clearly what we hoped that children would achieve through work in science. This involved saying what we meant by science for children whose ages ranged from five to thirteen years, who varied in capability from less than normal to very able, and in educational development from still thinking intuitively to thinking with the aid of abstractions. Further we had to make these statements against the background of our own educational convictions, namely that:

In general, children work best when trying to find answers to problems that they have themselves chosen to investigate.

These problems are best drawn from their own environment and tackled largely by practical investigations.

Teachers should be responsible for thinking out and putting into practice the work of their own classes.

In order to do so they should be able to find help where they need it.

The process of formulating these statements, however incompletely, we found uncomfortable, because it meant facing up to issues in general education that we would have preferred to leave for someone else; but the study of these issues did clarify our minds and we were glad to have attempted it. In doing so we sought the aid of teachers in discussion-groups and in teachers' centres. In the course of discussions it became clear that this process of clarifying our minds, so valuable to us, was also of help to the teachers whose aid we sought. Through discussion they began to reach conclusions of their own, not always the same as ours, though there was much in common, but which were more directly related to their own circumstances. They urged us to write about our conclusions and the way in which we reached them, not so that they could follow us to the same ends, but rather that they might have something to help them in making their own assessments.

Our problems were thus resolved into finding answers to the following three important questions:

1. What kind of science is right for children?

2. What do we want them to achieve through learning about science?

3. How can we best help them achieve it?

This book, then, is a discussion of the three major questions we encountered when we started, and it is supported by other books * in which the discussion is carried into the day-to-day work that children and teachers do together.

* See the Appendix, page 55.

4

What kind of science is right for children?

Science often means different things to different people. To some it means research, or perhaps the pursuit of truth, whatever that is ; to some it is developing technology intended to benefit mankind ; to some it is finding out, experimenting, measuring ; and to others it is extending the authenticated description of the physical world. It seems unlikely that someone engaged in science will pursue all these ends at the same time, but rather that he will be involved in one activity, or perhaps a few of them. He is likely to be engaged in different aspects of science at different periods of his life.

Our purpose here is to say what we think science means to children between the ages of five and thirteen years. Exploration of the environment is certainly involved—the examination of what is there—and this is an activity in which all teachers can help, whether they are trained in science or not ; all have experience of an environment that they can share with the children. There may be experimenting, there may be measuring, but much of the work will be finding out.

What ways of finding out or of exploring are suited to children between the ages of five and thirteen ? This is a question that cannot be resolved easily or shortly ; indeed, the answers we suggest will emerge piecemeal throughout the rest of this book. Ways of exploring that are appropriate to a child of thirteen are not likely to be those that suit a child of five ; nor are ways that suit one child of thirteen bound to be those that suit another. Children of the same age probably have different mental capacities, and those capacities that they each have may be well or ill developed. We are plunged at the outset into considering what these differences are and how they emerge in the course of children's development. Much has been written on this subject, and it is for us to select from it what is relevant to the field we are studying.

There are, however, certain preliminary conclusions that we can reach before we embark on a detailed consideration of how children develop and how their development affects their way of working. We have said that science involves exploration, and exploration involves the gathering of experience—a process that goes on throughout our lives. We can certainly help children to gather appropriate experience of their environment, and our convictions are that we must help them to ask their own questions and find their own answers by first-hand investigation as far as may be. They will organise their experience into some pattern personal to themselves, and we can help them to do so through discussion, but we must be careful that our own ideas about science and our own ideas of what they might achieve through it do not dull our perception of the individual natures of these children and what they need to develop their different potentials.

For instance, part of science is concerned with ordering experiences into a structure and extending that structure by making hypotheses* about causes and effects which then we proceed to look for. This is fine, but if in our work with children our hypotheses and our examination of cause and effect lead us to make generalisations that depend upon abstractions, we shall have done no service to those of our children who cannot yet think in the abstract. For them we had far better stick to actual things and to the properties we observe that those things have. Most of our children will be happier talking about the speed of cars, falling stones and moving planets than about velocity and acceleration which are abstractions drawn from experience of moving objects. This is not to say that there will not be some who are ready for work that calls for the power to make abstractions : among our older and abler children there well may be, but we shall need to know who they are, and

---

In science, hypotheses are suppositions put forward to account for known facts and to serve as starting points for further investigations through which they may be proved or disproved.

to be sure they have the powers that this kind of work demands. To a discerning teacher those who have such powers, and those who have not, reveal themselves through the kind of problem that they choose themselves to tackle, and the kind of answer they propound. To some teachers such an analysis of pupils' powers may be carried out by intuition. Even so, most teachers will be helped by studying the factors involved in the problem of suiting work to individual children.

What do we want children to achieve through science?

Much of what we want them to achieve through science will be similar to, if not the same as, what we hope they will achieve through work in other subjects. The younger the children the more similar these sets of aims will be, for boundaries between some subject areas will scarcely yet be formed. It is at the later stages that efforts to fulfil our aims will need the support of subject material that is placed more recognisably in the field of science.

The aims that we have may thus be of a general kind in the first instance, but if they are to be useful in planning day-to-day work in what we broadly call science, we must add to them others that are sufficiently specific for the purpose. This was a task that occupied us for some time; eventually, by a process that is described later in this book,* we arrived at what we called a guide to *Objectives for children learning science.*†

In considering what might be suitable objectives for children learning science the same danger signals appear regarding what they might achieve that we noted in the previous section, less prominently perhaps if the aims are our own

* *See pages 21-23 and Chapter 4.*
† *See page 59.*

than if they stem from someone else. But from whatever source they are derived, if we set up specific aims and work to them slavishly they could get between us and our children and so lessen our sensitivity to these children's needs : we could be blinded by our own intentions. (An illustration of how this situation was avoided is to be found in Chapter 2, page 15.) But some of our aims can still be specific if we remember that our hopes for children's achievements must be kept in perspective against the needs that children reveal as we work with them. These needs we must try first to perceive and then to satisfy. So then, if broad aims do not give sufficient guidance we must fine down objectives in ways that will permit us to allow both for the educational development that takes place in children as they grow, and for the differences that remain among individuals as they do so. This operation of refining aims needs a detailed study that will be undertaken in Chapter 3.

There is, however, another consideration that must not be overlooked : it is this. As things are now, and as they are likely to be for many years to come, the groups in which children are taught contain individuals who, though they may be of the same chronological age, may well be at different stages of educational development. This kind of grouping has many advantages, but it poses problems for a teacher who must help all children in the group to work so that each develops his own potential powers; this leads us to our third big question.

How can we help them achieve their own potential?

This Project aims at helping children through helping teachers. It tries to help teachers by encouraging them to think critically and profitably about their own work and to develop it as best suits their own children, their own powers and their own circumstances. For this purpose a course, a package of apparatus or a kit of parts would be too limiting : the help that is offered must be such as can be adapted to particular circumstances in situations that are as child-centred as may be. It must be such as to encourage teachers to put children in situations that stimulate them to ask questions and to undertake activities likely to provide answers. It must be such as helps teachers to make use of what is likely to be found in a school environment, and to reveal its possibilities as material for investigation. It must provide some insight as to how investigations may be conducted, give support when they are undertaken, and yet leave elbow-room for both teachers and children to do their own thinking and draw their own conclusions.

Help of this kind can be given if children work in small groups or as individuals in areas of study that, preferably, they have themselves chosen.

We therefore studied some of these areas with children and teachers, and, having identified some of the possible objectives, suggested experiences that might help the children achieve these objectives through their own efforts, guided in part by the teacher. But we did not stop there ; we presented these studies in ways aimed at encouraging teachers to identify and work towards other objectives that might emerge through the children's work and that were personal to both children and teacher. These studies we called 'Units' ; we wrote them up in the form of booklets and added to some of them booklets of background information for teachers where such information was hard to come by : a list of those written so far is given in the Appendix. The discussion of these Units is taken up again in Chapter 5.

For work in Infants' schools we looked at what teachers and children actually did together in classrooms, identified points relevant to a continued education in science, and collected them together in one book called *Early experiences*. The teachers themselves were mostly unaware that these activities were related to science or indeed to each other : they were

glad to have pointed out to them links in their work that they did not know existed ; furthermore they saw a pattern (of objectives) that enabled them to make profitable extensions of what they already did.

The link between these Units is the guide to *Objectives for children learning science.*
It is true, as we have already pointed out, that there are certain dangers about having objectives that are closely specified ; they may, for instance, be so detailed or so inflexible that they leave no elbow-room for either teacher or child. The position is summed up in two quotations, both from the same book, 'I've always thought that to define the aims of education in general terms is more or less meaningless ; to do it more precisely is downright dangerous.' * 'I am under no illusions about the difficulties of translating into action any high-sounding statement of aims and objectives. But these difficulties are minimal compared to the problems which the absence of such a guide creates.'† Thus a position of some delicacy has to be established. The objectives, whatever they are, must not intervene between teacher and pupil ; they must be present in the teacher's mind, but not so far in the forefront of it that she sees them rather than the children and the ways in which she can meet their needs. It would be idle to pretend that such a position could be established through the printed word alone, but print supported by discussion and critical personal appraisal might do much. The Science 5/13 Project is trying to establish these conditions in as wide and realistic a manner as circumstances permit.

The position we have come to, then, is this :

1. Science work based on logical propositions is best deferred until children have developed some ability to think in the abstract.

---

* Curriculum Innovation in Practice, *Schools Council, HMSO, 1968, page 4.*
† Ibid, *page 13.*

2. Until that stage is developed, children could be helped through investigations to gather experience of their environment and, where appropriate, to organise it themselves into small areas of development, to be joined up later.

3. It is possible to pursue such a course profitably, guided by suitable objectives, so that individually and in groups children work at their own pace and at their own level.

4. Attitudes of enquiry, objective judgement, personal responsibility, ability to work independently and organise one's own work can be established in children at an early age, though the subject-matter through which these attitudes are encouraged may well not be prearranged in detail by the teacher.

2 Children developing

Describing the changes

In this chapter we look at the children. We wish to
help them along the course of their development
so that they may achieve as much as possible
of their potential throughout this development.
To do this we must be aware of the path it seems
to take.

The ideas and abilities of children change
enormously between the ages of five and
thirteen, more than they will change during any
span of eight years later in their lives. These
changes are gradual and continuous ; we might
picture them like this :

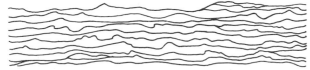

Each wavy line might be thought of as indicating
the development of a concept or the growth of an
idea or the progress towards some skill or ability.
There would be a very great many such lines, or
strands of development ; we show only a few
here so that their form might indicate some of the
characteristics we believe children's mental
development has :

a. The strands do not run in parallel straight
lines ; their waviness is meant to indicate that
development does not always take place in what
we think of as a forward direction.

b. Two or more strands may meet, where separate
ideas become amalgamated into a more general idea.

c. One strand may divide into two or more,
when ideas become more specific.

Of course the details of these strands of
development vary from one individual to
another, but Piaget's* work has shown that it is
possible to discern a pattern in them which is
similar for different individuals. Piaget has found
that all children pass through a stage in which
their thought processes are described as

*Jean Piaget (1896–), a Swiss professor, has
been investigating since the early 1920s many
aspects of the development of children's
thought. Until recently he worked in Geneva and
is still publishing his findings; the work he has
done, or inspired, constitutes a very large
proportion of all that has ever been done in this
field.

'pre-operational', then into a stage where thought is 'concrete operational', before reaching the 'formal operational' stage of thought. Piaget found that children pass through these stages in this order but at a rate which varies from child to child.

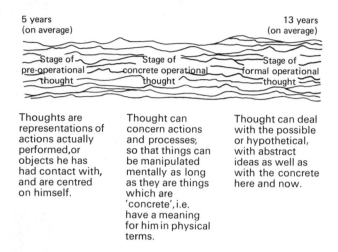

5 years (on average)

13 years (on average)

Stage of pre-operational thought

Stage of concrete operational thought

Stage of formal operational thought

Thoughts are representations of actions actually performed, or objects he has had contact with, and are centred on himself.

Thought can concern actions and processes; so that things can be manipulated mentally as long as they are things which are 'concrete', i.e. have a meaning for him in physical terms.

Thought can deal with the possible or hypothetical, with abstract ideas as well as with the concrete here and now.

The description of certain parts of children's development as 'stages' is merely a convenience, it does not imply that the development is thought of as taking place in a series of hops. The development is a continuous process with labels attached at certain points simply to make reference more easy. In theory suitable labels could be attached to any parts of it, but Piaget has good reasons for choosing these particular ones.

What Science 5/13 'Stages' mean

We have also found it useful to describe development in terms of stages; we call them Stages 1, 2 and 3. Our Stages are chosen so as to divide the development in the period with which we are concerned into three more convenient parts than would have been the case had we kept to Piaget's stages. Since we follow quite closely Piaget's ideas about development our Stages 1, 2 and 3 have similar properties to

Piaget's stages, namely:

a. Each Stage extends and builds upon the one before and then forms the necessary foundation for the next Stage.

b. Children pass through these Stages in the same order 1 → 2 → 3, though the rate at which they pass through them varies between individuals.

c. Age is no guide to Stage for a particular child. It is only when referring to the average of a large number of children that Stage can be roughly related to age.

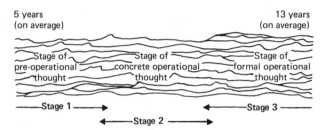

5 years (on average)

13 years (on average)

Stage of pre-operational thought

Stage of concrete operational thought

Stage of formal operational thought

Stage 1 → ← Stage 2 → ← Stage 3

Stage 1
This part of development includes some pre-operational and some concrete operational thought, but chiefly the transition between the two. Generally Infants are in the first half of this Stage, where thought is 'intuitive', closely associated with physical action and dominated by immediate observation. Infants often cannot foresee the consequences of an action unless they have actually carried it out; they are not likely to draw logical conclusions from their experiences. Children in the second half of this Stage are developing the ability to manipulate things mentally. At first the mental operations are not only restricted to dealing with 'concrete', real things, but are restricted in extent.

Stage 2
In this part of development concrete operational thought is well established and is the main way of thinking. Mental manipulations are becoming more varied and powerful. The whole of a

process, including its reverse, can be envisaged; the idea of conservation of physical quantities develops. The growth of ability to handle variables means that problems can be solved in more ordered and quantitative ways than was possible previously. But all this is still with reference to things or situations with a real meaning in physical terms. The properties of things are not distinguished from the things which have them; objects tend to be defined in terms of what they can do or what one can do with them, not so much in terms of their form.

Stage 3

In this part of development children are in transition from concrete operational to formal operational thought. Formal thought is characterised by abilities, not previously possible, which derive from the power to think about what is abstract and not only what is actual. Some of these abilities are: to hypothesise, * to think about what is possible but not observable, to extrapolate beyond experience, to consider the spatially remote, to extract a principle from various examples of it, to generalise, to draw

* See pages 5 and 43 for an explanation of this term.

conclusions, to apply knowledge where it is necessary first to decide what knowledge is relevant, to deal with variables in all, not just some, of their possible combinations. These abilities develop slowly over many years. In Stage 3 children are just beginning this development; the formal operational abilities will not generally appear until after the age of thirteen.

This is very condensed and generalised: some examples of how the differences between one Stage and another are illustrated by children's work may help to give them meaning.

'Concrete' experience in an Infants' class involves using materials and so exploring them for a purpose; the children are becoming aware of similarities and differences between materials by handling and working on them. The resulting structure is itself one form of record of their discoveries

This is a girl putting her hands on her ears so that is not her voice so loud

Infants begin by looking at things from one point of view—their own, which can lead to confusion of cause and effect

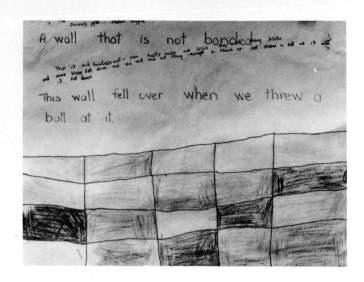

A wall that is not bonded

This wall fell over when we threw a ball at it.

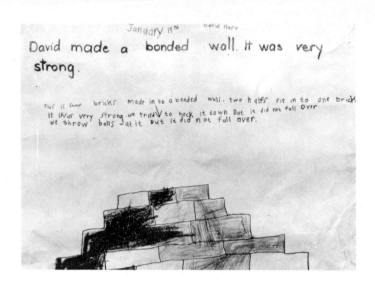

January 19th   David Hart

David made a bonded wall. It was very strong.

Learning by 'seeing what happens'. This work by older Infants is typical of Stage 1

Children watching to see if a snail prefers damp or dry soil. But is it a fair test? There are many differences between the two soils besides the dampness which these children have not noticed. In this respect they are still at Stage 1

More of the variables are controlled in this comparison of the bendiness of different knitting needles. This and the use of measurement to aid interpretation of observations is typical of Stage 2

The children who set up this experiment to find out the conditions which minibeasts prefer succeeded in separating and combining the variables under investigation—the amount of dampness and of light—and in keeping all other conditions the same. Their ability to think about the various possibilities and to plan out such an experiment indicates that these top juniors were at Stage 3 in this area of their experience

Individual children and Stages

The diagram on page 10 gives a rough indication of an *average* age/Stage relationship, but this is no guide for individual children or even for particular whole classes.

In particular cases it is the succession of Stages which is important. We might summarise the position as follows:

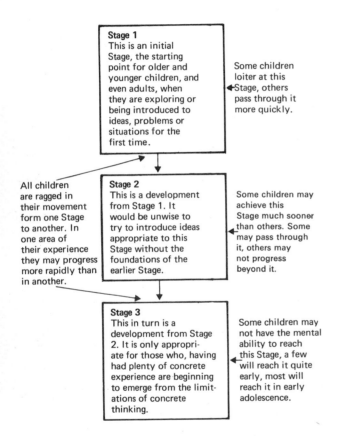

Stage 1
This is an initial Stage, the starting point for older and younger children, and even adults, when they are exploring or being introduced to ideas, problems or situations for the first time.

Some children loiter at this Stage, others pass through it more quickly.

All children are ragged in their movement form one Stage to another. In one area of their experience they may progress more rapidly than in another.

Stage 2
This is a development from Stage 1. It would be unwise to try to introduce ideas appropriate to this Stage without the foundations of the earlier Stage.

Some children may achieve this Stage much sooner than others. Some may pass through it, others may not progress beyond it.

Stage 3
This in turn is a development from Stage 2. It is only appropriate for those who, having had plenty of concrete experience are beginning to emerge from the limitations of concrete thinking.

Some children may not have the mental ability to reach this Stage, a few will reach it quite early, most will reach it in early adolescence.

We have said all this about children's development because it is our philosophy that the best learning will come from working with the tide of natural changes.

We hold that by enabling children to have experiences suited to their abilities at the time we help them to extend these abilities and eventually transform them into more advanced forms.

It is likely that children progress from one mode of thought to another by a series of constant adjustments of their ways of thinking. (Piaget calls this process 'accommodation'.) For instance, a child at the pre-operational stage is, for quite a while, satisfied with considering only one aspect of a thing at a time and with looking at things from only one point of view, his own. But eventually experience makes him aware of the inconsistencies in judgements and the ambiguities which this way of thinking inevitably involves. He is no longer able to make sense of his surroundings without adjusting his mode of thought, and gradually these adjustments lead to operational thought.

Later the child becomes more and more proficient at using the concrete operational methods which he elaborates and manipulates to their limits. As he does so he again becomes limited by the shortcomings of these methods which are tedious to apply in complex situations, particularly where there are several variables involved in solving a problem. Concrete operational thought leaves gaps in the investigation of combinations of variables, and often presents uncertainties and contradictions. When these restrictions are revealed by experience the child begins to adjust his methods and so the transition to formal operational thought begins.

A situation described by A. E. Peel is a typical one in which the progression from concrete to formal based thinking would be evident. A child who has a model train circuit powered from the electricity mains by a transformer finds that the train won't move when everything is plugged in and switched on. At the concrete operational stage he would try one remedy after another at random and if he found the fault it would probably be by luck. When this inefficient method has been outgrown, thought about the possibilities in the situation precedes action and then 'he will proceed systematically first checking the main, then the plug, then the transformer connections, then the switch gear, then the plug on to the rails, then the rail fittings and finally the "shoes" on different engines—thus eliminating one factor after another whilst the rest are held constant'. *

Matching learning experiences to stage of development

The part which experience plays in bringing about these changes is evidently an important one. With appropriate experiences the change from one form of thinking to another will take place more readily than without them. Such experiences must ideally be not only well suited to a child's point of mental development but also ones which are interesting and real to him, so we think it best if children have a large part in choosing the problems they work on and so in the experience they gather. But, of course, their range of choice is determined by what the teacher makes available to them and their progress depends largely on the guidance they get from her. Thus it is important for her to have some idea of the stage of development of each child in relation to any particular topic or set of problems, and to be able to find suggestions, if she needs them, for suitable activities.

We do not want children to 'mark time' on activities which are insufficiently challenging for them; but the opposite mistake is probably more common and damaging, when children are introduced to ideas or expected to deal with problems for which they are not ready, that is to say they have not yet reached the stage of development required to cope with the thinking that the problem requires. The assumption that necessary concepts have been fully formed, when this is not the case, can lead to children losing interest or uncomprehendingly following

instructions. The danger is present at all stages, but is probably greatest in Stage 3 at the transition from concrete operational to formal thinking. It takes longer for this transition to take place than we sometimes make allowances for, and we often forget that some children never reach this stage at all. When a house is built on a shaky foundation it is impossible to feel comfortable in it and given a chance a person is likely to stay in it as little as possible. So with formal science; if it is erected on an inadequate foundation of earlier experiences it is probably avoided at the first opportunity.

There will be many children who reach the secondary stage of schooling without having formed ideas about conservation of various kinds of quantity, about cause and effect, about the nature of measurement, about classification and many other concepts which, had the opportunity been provided, they might have developed in earlier years. If the secondary work presupposes that such ideas have been grasped when in fact they have not, the children's appreciation of much of the work that follows is blocked from the start.

A first-year mixed-ability class in a comprehensive school was being introduced to some work on materials. The teacher was hoping that the work would lead to appreciation that ways in which materials are used depend on their properties. However, she soon realised that before there was any hope of this idea being appreciated the children needed opportunity, which they had not had previously, to collect, examine, bang about and generally become acquainted with different materials and to discover their properties at first hand. They also needed to identify the materials in use around them and the chance to consider the uses of materials before they could arrive at the idea that the uses might be influenced by the properties. The class described some of the work at first as 'little kid's stuff', but they enjoyed it none the less. They felt free to ask simple questions and, as their progress was rapid, the work was especially satisfying. They found, with some relief, that 'science' was not going to be as frightening and incomprehensible as some older children had led them to believe.

* *A. E. Peel,* The Pupil's Thinking, *revised edition, 1967, London, Oldbourne.*

It is easy to see how this teacher could have persisted with her original plan had she not noticed the signs of the children not being ready for it. It is not only in the secondary school that a teacher can make the mistake of assuming that necessary ideas have already been formed, instead of looking for signs of whether they have or have not.

Recognising children's stages of development

It is all very well to urge that children's science experience should match their stages of development in scientific ideas, but this is no easy task for a teacher. There are two sides to the problem : one is to be able to recognise the stage a particular child has reached with respect to a certain area of experience, and the other is to know what kind of activity is suited to this stage of development. Only when these two things are known can 'matching' take place.

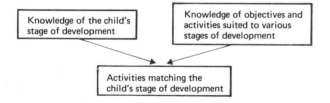

The Science 5/13 Project is trying to give teachers help with both the processes involved in 'matching'. The Units give guidance as to objectives and activities which are appropriate at a particular Stage ; different Units attempt to provide this help in different ways. From the description of the children's thinking at various stages of development in this book, and in summaries in each Unit, teachers may already find some help with recognising the Stages reached by their children. We realise however that many teachers would like more help than is given by these broad outlines. The Project attempted to give more detailed guidance to the identification of Stages by providing diagnostic statements. The statements help to direct teachers' observation to things that children may or may not do which would be indicative of the Stages reached by the children. They were tried out by over 300 teachers ; the results were encouraging, but revealed the need for considerable further development. The necessary additional work was much greater than could be undertaken by Science 5/13, so the Schools Council set up a new project called 'Progress in learning science' beginning in 1973, to work on the production of materials aimed at helping teachers observe and record the development of their children's ideas and concepts in relation to science.

3 The contribution of science to early education

What is the point of science in the primary school?

A teacher recording her work in pilot-trials of one of our first Units wrote:

'This is not the science of the secondary. It is concerned with widening the child's sphere of experience rather than with treating particular topics in readiness for a secondary stage of education . . . The emphasis must always be on the children and their growth and development as individuals, for we should be teaching the whole child. We are not teaching science, at least I am not. I am using their interests and developing personalities as vehicles for learning.'

This expresses a theme which runs through our Project, that science activities in the primary school have a vital contribution to make to the 'whole' education of children, a contribution that has very little to do with the acquisition of scientific knowledge or with the subject 'science' in the secondary school. As was pointed out in Chapter 1, page 5, science can mean many things, and in the early years of school at least, 'exploration' would be a more appropriate title.

But saying what primary science is *not* is hardly helpful to those who want to know what it *is*. That it is 'concerned with widening the child's sphere of experience' is a first step towards an answer—but only a first step, because this would be among the aims of activities in all areas of the curriculum, and it gives no indication of the particular contribution science activities can make

to the achievement of educational aims. The teacher quoted above went on to say what she meant by this statement in less general terms which were more relevant to everyday events in the classroom.

This is an ideal situation, when a teacher works out for herself a personal statement of her aims. But we realise that there are very many teachers who do not feel equipped by their training or experience to do this in the area of science activities; those who do may like to compare their ideas with what others think.

The value of working out aims

Teachers may find that an answer worked out in some detail to the question at the beginning of this chapter is an effective form of help, because:

a. Having some idea of what are worthwhile aims means that one can find satisfaction in working towards them. Nothing which seems 'aimless' or 'pointless' can bring the sense of achievement which is both satisfying and which provides motivation for further work.

A 'non-scientific' teacher, writing about using the Unit *Working with wood* which introduced her to the Project, said: 'We could go on and on and on. Each day brings a new interest—a new discovery.' Another said that the explicit discussion of aims made it 'easier to think of starting points and gain my own confidence in the worthwhileness of science activities'.

b. Clarifying aims can in itself make the

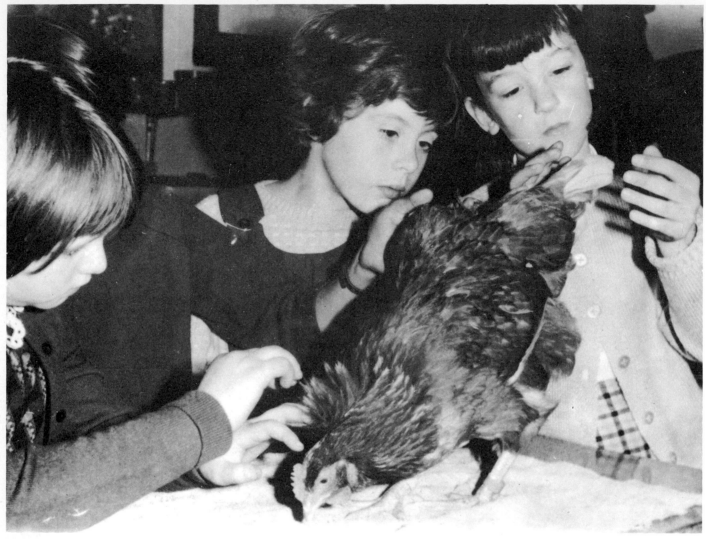

'It is concerned with widening the child's sphere of experience'

achievement of the aims more likely.

In this connection a teacher wrote: 'I have not much scientific knowledge myself. This [indication of aims and objectives] has helped to pin ideas down.'

c. With aims consciously in mind one may be able to ensure that there is purpose in what the children do and may have a better chance of

ensuring that the children get good value from their activities.

Here is a teacher with aims in mind: 'We started to discuss ways by which we could see which woods were harder than others. I was amazed at the suggestions offered by the children, as I will admit to having been rather sceptical in the past when I read the Teachers' Unit [*Working with wood*]. Rather than note them all down myself

I gave the children the chance to write down the ideas they had suggested. Deliberately I gave the children a piece of wood to lean on when writing, and Graeme (an intelligent boy) told us that if anybody's leaning board was of soft wood, markings would be left after the pencil and paper were removed. The children proved remarkably perceptive . . .'

This third point seems particularly relevant to situations where children are learning through exploration and are concerned with finding answers to the questions which are important to them. In such situations they are doing much more than adding to their factual knowledge, they are also developing attitudes, skills, basic concepts, the ability to devise ways of testing their ideas and solving the problems they have found. The children, concentrating on their discoveries and on achieving their immediate aims, are hardly conscious of what they are gaining in these other ways; but they will be gaining in them just as well, and much less uncomfortably, than if they were learning by rote

'Having fun and learning too'

and being all too conscious of doing so. Their teacher, on the other hand, must be very much aware of the potential for children's learning in any experience she makes available to them, and must be sure to take as much advantage of it as possible. In practice this may mean only a word here, a question there, throwing a child's question back instead of supplying an easy answer, providing material at the right time to suggest a particular use for it or to provoke curiosity, and so on. These are the things which can make the difference between a restricted 'closed' enquiry and a developing 'open' one that branches out into many fields of activity. They are important ways of guiding the children's work which can easily be overlooked unless prompted by specific aims in the teacher's mind.

A series of activities which gave a group of four children a variety of profitable experience was started off, in the teacher's words, like this:

'In the original collecting (for a display of different metals) I had taken a piece of lead and hammered one half of it out quite a bit. Beside it I had left the hammer. Occasionally the more adventurous had a bang at it. Lorraine was first to approach me, saying how much wider one side had become. John (trying to impress both of us) said he thought he could make it twice as big. Doreen, Lorraine's friend and Jim, John's friend, became involved and the four decided to have a competition. I waited hopefully as they began to search for bits of lead. Soon they were back, saying there were no two pieces the same size.

' . . . a word here, a question there . . .'

20

It would not be fair if one piece were big and one were small.'

The teacher provided a large piece of lead which the children sawed into four, but 'Lorraine felt her piece was slightly smaller than the others and placed it over Doreen's. From this all four decided they needed to record the size before hammering started.' Their efforts to compare areas led them to the need for measurement and a great deal of mathematics was done, and, of course 'Doreen and Lorraine became interested to find out if they could flatten and widen other metals. They have raided the collection. . . .'

Children have a well-developed idea of what is and what is not 'fair' in a variety of situations. A teacher can use this as a start for discussing what being 'fair' means. 'Fairness' probably means giving things or people an equal chance, keeping constant the conditions which can change. When children begin to notice what can change they are identifying the variables and making an important step towards controlling and investigating variables. **Being able to make a fair test is fundamental to a scientific approach to problems but its importance is far from being restricted to science activities. Encouraging children to be on the look-out for whether or not the test they apply or a claim they make is fair will benefit their reasoning in almost all areas of their experience.**

The broad aims

For aims to be useful in these ways they have to be fairly specific. Very general statements, which summarise a certain philosophy of education, can have little influence on day-to-day work in the classroom. So, although it is important to state our idea of the general aim of science activities for young children, we realise that of itself its only value is in expressing our child-centred philosophy in early science teaching.

This aim, arrived at through discussions with teachers and others with wide and relevant experience, is: **developing an enquiring mind and a scientific approach to problems.**

This statement has been broken down into less general and more practical ones by trying to answer questions which teachers must ask if they want to make use of it in practice, questions such as:

What is meant by an enquiring mind?
Does it mean the same thing for children at different stages of development?
What is involved in a scientific approach?
and so on.

In the first step of this process we arrived at eight broad aims which indicate, still in general terms, what the statement implies for children at any stage of development.

This was the result:

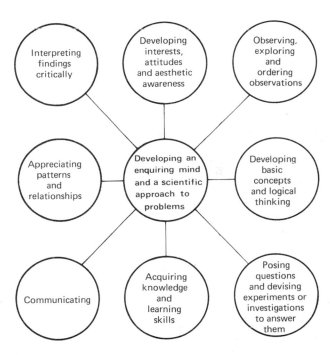

Arriving at objectives

In the second step of breaking down our general aim the process of trying to answer the awkward questions continued:

What abilities, skills, interests, attitudes, are most appropriately developed at particular stages?

What does this general aim mean in terms of changes in children?

In what respects does a child who has developed an enquiring mind differ from one who has not?

How will you know when an aim has been achieved?

Unless a set of aims enables questions of this kind to be answered the aims are unlikely to be useful in practice. Having an aim cannot lead to satisfaction unless it is possible to recognise its achievement. So aims are most effective when they are expressed in terms of expected changes in children, and changes which can be observed. This means that where possible they must indicate changes in what children can do, in what opinions they express, in their preferences, in their skills—in other words in their 'behaviour', where this word is used in its technical sense, meaning all the various kinds of response a person can make.

Expressed in this way, in terms of recognisable changes in behaviour, the aims are generally described as 'operational', or 'behavioural' objectives. When we refer to our objectives it is this kind of statement we mean. For instance:

'Experimenting with different materials.

This is an aim *not* expressed in behavioural terms.

It indicates *how* we intend to deal with the study of materials but not *why* we are doing it or what it is that we hope to achieve.

An objective does the reverse: it indicates *why* but not *how*.

To turn this aim into an objective requires a little more thinking in order to decide just why we wish our children to experiment with materials. What do we hope they will achieve through doing so? According to the previous experience and stage of development of the children, the answer might be that we hope they will gain:

Appreciation of the variety of materials in the environment.

or

Ability to discriminate between different materials.

or

Awareness that there are various ways of testing out ideas and making observations.

or

Appreciation that the properties of materials influence their uses.

or any combination of these or other objectives.

These are statements which **indicate the outcome, but do not prescribe the means of reaching it.**

Of course one could follow up with more questions:

Which materials?

Which properties?

leading to a very large number of specific statements. We had to decide where to stop.

Being firmly of the opinion that it is for teachers to decide what is best suited to their children, we stopped well before the statements became so detailed as to prescribe exactly what a child should know and do, before the statements began to refer not only to *why*, but also to *what, when* and *how*. We tried to avoid the error of being, on the one hand, too general to be useful and, on the other, too specific to be good for the children.

How objectives can be useful

Because objectives are aims expressed in a particular way they can be of help, as already suggested in our discussion of aims (page 17) ; but they can also be useful in other ways, because they are more specific and practical. Some of these particular advantages of working with objectives in mind are revealed in the following examples.

An experienced teacher of children aged seven to nine years in a country school, planning a morning's walk with her class to a nearby wood, chose carefully the part of the wood to be visited. Walking in the wood was not a new experience for the children, but on this day the teacher made sure that there would be opportunity to notice and explore fresh and exciting features. This time they walked through some dense parts of the wood and also through large green clearings which, in itself, encouraged the children to question why there were green spaces, why certain trees had fallen, why some trees were taller than others, how much taller they were and why it was so much wetter under the trees than

in the clearings. It rained on the day she took them; the teacher commented afterwards 'I recommend a wet, dripping wood for the greatest interest', and she went on in her notes 'The children were allowed to collect anything they wished—provided that they had some reason for the collection.' These collections included rotting wood, fungi, leaf mould, a large saturated log, rocks and fossils, and many other things, all of which were very thoroughly observed or used later in the classroom, as would be expected since the children had definite purposes for what they gathered. They brought something else back too, because, again in the teacher's words, 'This walk

resulted in good free-expression writing about the "feel" of the wood that day. Children who usually said little had lots to say in the class discussion.'

Evidently the teacher had thought in some detail about the potential which this occasion would hold for adding to the children's experience in many ways. This did not mean, as we have seen, that she had decided exactly what the children should collect and observe, rather it meant that the children discovered things which they might otherwise have missed.

Not all the objectives this teacher had for the children were concerned with science, of course, but if we confine ourselves to discussion of the ones which were, it is likely that these were the main ones :

An eleven-year-old boy became intrigued by a little wooden boat displayed in his classroom. The teacher describes what this led to. 'He said he would like to make one and asked which wood was best. I didn't know (as usual). His two friends suggested that Robert had found white pine the best for carving but I said that it may not be best for floating.' This was enough to start two groups on comparing the floating of different woods. Later, 'I had a look at the results of the two floating experiments. The amazing thing about them is that they are working completely apart yet (in different ways) they are really measuring the displacement of water. They talk in one group of measuring the water "pushed out" by the wood—this group have linked their experiment to the weight of the woods. In the other they have measured the rise in level of the water when different woods have been floated—

Willingness to collect materials for observation or investigation and *Sensitivity to the need for giving proper care to living things*		in making their collections
Appreciation of the need for measurement	—	when comparing heights of trees
Development of a concept of environment	—	through considering the differences between dense and open parts of the wood
Awareness of change in living things and non-living materials	—	in comparing the old, fallen trees and rotting wood with the younger trees and wood

On another occasion a walk in the same wood could help towards achieving other things, in which case the teacher would draw attention to different features, ask, and encourage the children to ask, different questions. The objectives would be different, but being conscious of them **helps the teacher to take advantage of the potential elements of science which are in any of their activities.**

their results were different. In the ensuing heated discussion group X convinced group Y that their results were more correct because three children had taken each measurement, thus double-checking results. Group Y accepted this and now are repeating.'

These children were trying to find out something which, as a piece of information was not very important and could easily have been obtained from reference books. If the 'success' of their activities were to have been gauged by their results then these activities would have been rated as unsuccessful. But it is evident that these were extremely successful activities in helping the children towards objectives such as:

Awareness that there are various ways of testing out ideas and making observations.

Development of a concept of volume.

Recognition of the role of chance in making measurements.

Ability to frame questions likely to be answered through investigations.

The teacher realised that it was far more important for the children to have experiences which helped towards achievement of these things than for them to find out exactly how much water each block of wood displaced.

In discovery situations there is often doubt as to whether the children will reach a result which seems 'right', and sometimes both teachers and children feel insecure when they are not sure of arriving at a 'good answer'. But, as the above quotation shows, when it is realised that important objectives can be achieved by making attempts to solve problems, regardless of whether the results are useful or not, then it is possible to feel much happier about embarking on these attempts. What we are suggesting is that **working with objectives takes some of the insecurity out of discovery situations.**

An extract from a teacher's account of working with the Unit *Time* during pilot trials:

'We were lucky with the weather this week and were able to do some [more] work with shadow sticks on the playground. When groups of children went out to have a look at shadows on the playground they noticed that the length and position of the shadow at a particular time of the day were not identical to the length and position that the shadow had been when previous work had been done. As a result of looking at these shadows, discussion followed on the movement of the sun. From these discussions much work was done on time of the day, day and night, and seasons. Groups of children devised experiments to try to explain the movement of the sun. After this, discussion followed and some book research.'

From simple observation and recording of shadows these children made considerable progress towards an appreciation of quite complex relationships. Of course this particular situation was not arranged in order to start work on day and night and the seasons, neither was this exact development suggested in the Unit. But what was suggested in the Unit was that teachers might keep in mind various objectives, one of which was:

Awareness of factors in the environment that change with the passage of time and ability to investigate these factors.

This teacher saw, in the situation he described, an opportunity to work towards this objective, and, being mentally prepared to take advantage of it, he encouraged progress in a useful direction. Perhaps this opportunity for making progress may have been missed had he not had the objective in mind: we cannot tell. We only know that, in this case, he did think it helped; which supports our view that **objectives have a value in encouraging progression in work.**

It is not only bright children who make progress, though theirs is quick and more obvious. Slower children, given time, can progress too. The same teacher goes on:

'Although this area of the work was difficult, some pleasing results were achieved. None was more pleasing than some observation work done by a 'none-too-bright' lad who sat for long periods of time looking at a world globe balanced in a flower-pot. He was shining a torch on the

27

globe which was in position with the two poles vertically above each other. During discussion with him it was obvious that he was beginning to work out how the earth came to have different seasons. However, things were still 'clouded' and observation continued. The next time I went to see how he was progressing he had tilted the globe so that the North Pole was away from the torch light. He explained that other children had got their earth tilted so he had done the same. He pointed out that the North Pole wouldn't get any light at all whilst in this position. After further discussion and suggestions and questions, this lad was well on his way to having a good grasp of the change of length of day and seasons.'

Here we have also a typical instance of a teacher being rewarded with considerable satisfaction from seeing children progress towards sound goals.

There must have been considerable satisfaction, too, for another teacher observing some of her children gaining *interest in discussing and comparing the aesthetic qualities of materials*, in this case wood:

'Every piece of wood and timber is being sanded. Several children see pictures in the polished graining. It is amazing to see the utter satisfaction the smooth wood gives to all the children. They touch it, hold it to their soft cheeks. I even saw Grace exploring the smooth surface with her tongue.'

How does working this way affect the children?

These cases illustrate some of the major advantages which teachers have found to result from thinking consciously about their objectives.

So far we have talked only of the teachers, but we have not forgotten that the children's interests come first. 'What is to the advantage of the children' is the criterion for deciding what is to the advantage of teachers. If teachers have more confidence and find increased satisfaction in their work, then the children are evidently going to benefit. This is illustrated particularly in the first example of the nature walk, page 23. A whole morning in a wood, in the rain, might well have dampened enthusiasm and disappointed the children, but the result was quite the reverse. It seems reasonable to suppose that this was largely because their activities were purposeful and that their teacher made a virtue of the inclement conditions; they had not only the satisfaction of collecting material to suit their immediate goals, but also the stimulation which would lead to achievement of longer-term objectives.

Perhaps the greatest benefit to the children in the long run may result from the efforts their teachers make to find out what are suitable objectives for them bearing in mind their stage of development. As we have said (Chapter 2), children develop intellectually at different rates, and it is widely acknowledged that age is no more than a very rough guide to stages of mental development.

A child who has missed early experiences of a particular kind which are needed to develop the concepts and ideas required for making sense of later experiences in science is not likely to be in a position to benefit from these later experiences. To assume that he is ready to benefit merely because he is of a certain age and general ability could be a serious mistake.

Thinking out objectives will not in itself prevent this mismatching from happening, but teachers who consider these objectives in relation to individual children are less likely to make the mistake. Such teachers will find out what ideas the children already have so as to frame objectives for them accordingly and they will therefore know how firm a foundation, if any, they have upon which to build. Awareness of these things can do much to prevent children being plunged into investigations before they have formed the basic concepts or ways of problem-solving needed to deal with work at that level.

4 Our selection of objectives for children learning science

Drafting the objectives

Breaking down our main aim to produce objectives which we hoped would be practical but not restricting, by the process described in Chapter 3, page 22, led to a tentative first list of statements. This then went through many cycles of revision:

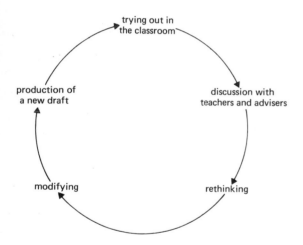

trying out in the classroom

discussion with teachers and advisers

rethinking

modifying

production of a new draft

The statements, their layout and the general form of the list have been changed many times in an attempt to make the result as useful as possible to teachers. The latest list, reproduced on pages 59–65, is the result of revision after the experience of extensive pilot trials as part of our first set of Units. We have more confidence in it than we had in the first drafts, but we know it is not 'right' and

never will be. Even after many revisions, past and future, the list will still be only one of a large number of possible selections.

The layout of the objectives

If you look on pages 59–65 you will see that the objectives in the list are arranged in eight groups under the broad aims to which they most relate. This is done mainly for convenience of handling a large number of statements. As in most groupings there are anomalies; some objectives appear to relate to more than one broad aim, some may seem to have been wrongly placed.

Within each of the eight groups the statements are divided into Stage 1, 2 and 3 objectives. This is because objectives that are to be of practical value have to take into account what children can reasonably be expected to achieve, and this obviously varies a great deal from the age of five to thirteen. The three Stages and our reasons for choosing them to help describe children's development have been discussed on pages 10 and 11 of Chapter 2.

We have already stressed that:

Previous experience and the grasp of particular ideas are what determine the appropriate Stages for individual children, not age.

Development is going on all the time; it does not take place through a series of steps.

Two things about the objectives follow from these points:

a. The objectives appropriate for children depend on their Stage of development, not on age.

b. The sequence of passing from one Stage to the next is best thought of as a cumulative process, with the objectives of earlier Stages persisting into later Stages.

The numbering system

The objectives in the list are numbered for easy reference. The numbers are simply labels; they do not convey an order of priority among the objectives.

The system of numbering is simple:

The *first* digit (1, 2 or 3)	indicates whether the objective is at Stage 1, 2 or 3.
The *second* digit	indicates the Broad Aim under which the objective is located.
The *third* digit	identifies the individual statement.

For example: the objective, *Ability to construct models as a means of recording observations* is numbered 2.74. This number has the following meaning:

2.74

2	7	4
This shows the Stage in children's development to which the objective chiefly applies — in this case **Stage 2**	This shows the broad aim to which the objective is expected to contribute — in this case **.70 Communicating**	This shows the position (arbitrary) in the list of Stage 2 Objectives that contribute to **Communicating**

Activities and objectives

A superficial glance at the list of objectives may give the impression that it is something like a syllabus. A closer look at any one of the statements will dispel this idea.

Partly because, as behavioural objectives, the statements are concerned with 'why' and not 'how', and partly because we deliberately did not analyse them further (see Chapter 3, page 22), the objectives have the following features:

a. They do not indicate to teachers anything about the materials or apparatus their children should use or about the experiments or activities they should undertake. Whether or not children achieve certain objectives in a situation in which these objectives potentially could be achieved depends on the way the situation is managed.

b. For children to achieve a particular objective it is not necessary for them all to have the same experiences, to perform the same experiments or to deal with the same problems. Each objective can be achieved in very many different ways, the choice being left to the teacher.

c. Teachers will find that the objectives we have selected are most easily and, in some cases only, achieved when children are actively investigating problems which are genuinely their own and are doing work which involves real discovery, with all the excitement and meaning this has for them.

d. Objectives at the level of generality of our statements are rarely achievable through a single activity or experience. Rather they are achieved as a result of prolonged exploration of the children's environment and of attempting to solve a range of problems.

There is no one way of achieving an objective. Achievement of objective X comes as a result of experience accumulated from several contributory activities:

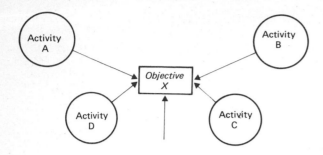

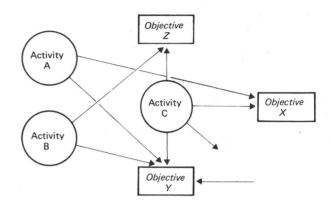

Instead it is nearer to being represented by a complex mesh :

In practice the situation is much more complicated than this, of course. A teacher will have many objectives for her children in mind at any one time, and in general there is potential for working towards several objectives through any one activity :

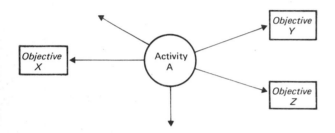

It follows that the relationship between objectives and activities is very far from being the simple one :

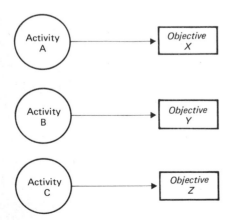

Evidently it is not a simple matter to envisage this relationship and we think it may help to have it illustrated in terms of real activities and objectives. One example is given in Chapter 2 of our Unit on Minibeasts. To give more examples we now take three objectives chosen at random and suggest activities from the Units which could contribute towards achieving them.

In the following diagram *some* of the activities in the Units which could help achieve this objective are picked out as examples. Whilst no one activity is sufficient for achieving a particular objective, we are not suggesting that all those in the diagram are necessary. They are in any case only a small proportion of the possibilities and simply illustrate that **there is a wide range of activities through which a particular objective can be achieved.**

Example 1
1.29 Ability to group living and non-living things by observable attributes
Although we are focusing upon objective 1.29 for the purpose of this example, it must not be forgotten that each activity contributing to this objective may contribute at the same time to others. For instance, if children were sorting metals the activity might also lead to :

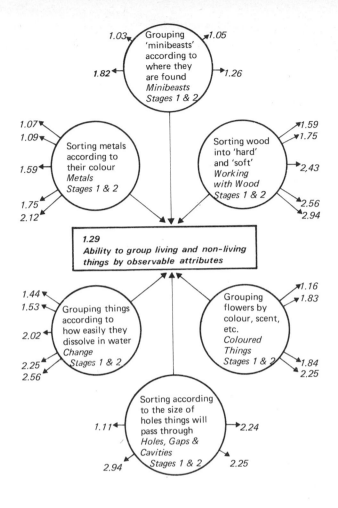

might add contribution towards:

1.16 Enjoyment in exploring the variety of living things in the environment.

1.83 Formation of a broad idea of variation in living things.

1.84 Awareness of seasonal changes in living things.

2.25 Ability to classify living things and non-living materials in different ways.

Some of these possibilities are indicated on the diagram by the reference number of the objectives to which the various activities might lead. Among these reference numbers are several beginning with 2.—indicating that they are Stage 2 objectives. This emphasises one of the advantages of thinking about the relationships between objectives and activities; that **it reveals the possibilities for achieving objectives at different Stages through working on the same subject matter.**

For instance, some of the children sorting wood into 'hard' and 'soft' may already have achieved *1.29* and could be encouraged to be more discriminating. They might try to arrange the woods in order of hardness (as suggested in the Unit) and to devise more sophisticated hardness tests for this purpose. These children could be working towards:

2.25 Ability to classify living things and non-living materials in different ways.

2.43 Appreciation of the need to control variables and use controls in investigations.

2.56 Knowledge of ways to investigate and measure properties of living things and non-living materials.

2.94 Recognition of the role of chance in making measurements and experiments.

1.07 Willing participation in group work.

1.09 Appreciation of the need to learn the meaning of new words and to use them correctly.

1.59 Knowledge of differences in properties between and within common group of materials.

1.75 Ability to tabulate and use tables.

Whilst grouping flowers according to colour, scent or other features the children's experience

Having identified these as potential objectives for children who have achieved the Stage 1 objectives in a particular activity makes it much easier to ensure that these children are progressing and not 'marking time'. This advantage of thinking about the relationships between objectives and activities, then, is that **it suggests ideas for progression towards more advanced objectives.**

The idea of variables is one which is central to a logical or scientific approach to problems. It is discussed in *Working with wood* and *Metals* in particular, but occurs in all the Units. Example 2 below may add to the clarification of the meaning of 'variables' in practical terms, as well as providing another example of the activity—objective relationships.

Example 2
2.42 Ability to investigate variables and to discover effective ones.

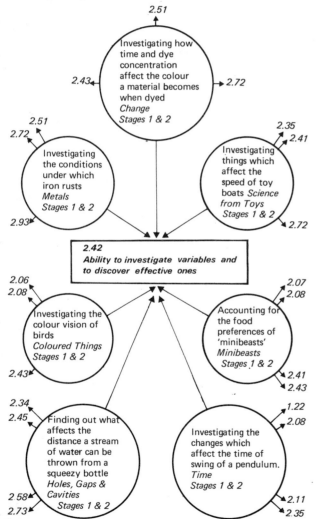

Example 3
1.92 Appreciation that properties of materials influence their use.

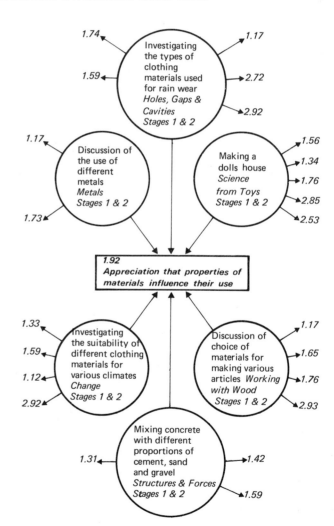

Extending the idea of working with objectives in mind

Many teachers have made use of our statement of objectives in a variety of ways apart from those connected with our Units for teachers. Some used them for planning other science work :

'In initiating a new topic in science, namely, Health.'

'We carried out a short study on a stream near the school and we approached the study in the same way as we did the Trees study.'

'In making judgements about the decisions on what other science work to give the children in the school ; for example, how valuable the BBC programmes are.'

Some used them in other areas of the curriculum :

'Planning my next project—Land Transport.'

'This statement of objectives is pertinent, not only to a study of science, but to all aspects of learning.'

'Maths—shapes from boxes with lids, rotation and symmetry.'

'It has made me try and apply similar principles to other work in the curriculum.'

'Given rise to staff discussion. Much can and has been useful in work in all subjects.'

This is what we hoped would happen, that teachers find the Project's ideas help them a great deal more than simply when they are using the Units :

At first using *our* objectives to help with other topics,

Eventually working out their *own* objectives for their children.

Some of our objectives, particularly at Stage 1, are indeed applicable to a much larger area of the curriculum than would normally be thought of as included in science. From the very large number of objectives that one might imagine to cover the curriculum we have had to select the ones that science activities can most effectively help children to achieve. The relationship between our selection and the other objectives of early education vary across the age range which concerns us. The objectives selected for Infant children are more general than those in the rest of the list. The activities which relate to science are spread throughout the general Infant activities and form an integral part of such occupations as water play, number games, making collections. For Infants science is indistinguishable as a separate activity and the objectives also relate to much more than 'scientific' ideas. The same is true for the rest of Stage 1, where the objectives refer to achievement which results from general exploration of the environment. Later, as children become capable of, and eager for, more sustained and ordered investigations, the objectives begin to relate more to science than to other fields of activity. The beginning of this can be seen at Stage 2, and it becomes more obvious at Stage 3. There is a gradual emergence of science as a recognisable activity and this is reflected in our selection of objectives.

The teacher who made use of our objectives in planning her topic Land Transport not only used our objectives to help her but also added some of her own. Her children were ten- to eleven-year-olds and had previously been working with her in pilot trials of the Project's Unit *Time*.

Work in all areas of the curriculum was encompassed by the topic, and since, as we have just said, our Stage 2 objectives are more restricted to science than those of the earlier Stage, they were not enough by themselves to guide all the activities this topic involved. Appropriate ones from our list both at Stage 1 and Stage 2 were selected by this teacher, and to these were added her own. For instance, under 'Developing interests, attitudes and aesthetic awareness':

'To be aware of the sound of words and to realise that sounds often convey meaning.

'To have their artistic awareness increased when viewing ordinary objects—the blueness in oiled steel—the colours in oil peacocked on roads—the patterns in tyres and railway lines.

'To have their perception heightened so that work in art, drama and writing is dynamic.'

Some of her objectives were more specific than ours. The job of breaking down the objectives further than we have is one we felt was not for us to do, but was for the teacher who knows the children (Chapter 3, page 22). Whether or not the objectives need to be broken down further, and if so, to what degree of specificity, varies between individual teachers. Some have found that our 'broad aims' give them all the guidance they need; others have found it useful to interpret our objectives in relation to the topic of the children's activities. In the case of 'Land Transport' the teacher wrote some quite specific objectives under 'Acquiring and applying knowledge':

'Knowledge of change of state of water.

'Knowledge of condensation and evaporation.

'Knowledge of power of steam.

'Knowledge of friction—where it helps and hinders.

'Knowledge of events leading to growth of roads and railways.'

Whether or not we agree with these particular statements is not the point at issue; rather it is whether or not it was a good thing for the teacher to have thought about what she hoped the children might get from the work. Our answer is an unqualified 'Yes'.

5 The Units, their development and use

Producing the Units

We said earlier, in Chapter 1, page 7, that we envisaged children working in small groups or as individuals in areas of study that, preferably, they had chosen for themselves. We said also that we proposed to help teachers bring about this desirable state of affairs by writing 'Units' for them, which are studies of subject-areas in which children might be likely to work, perhaps stimulated by their teacher to do so. **These Units do not in any way constitute a course or even part of a course. They are illustrations of ways in which a teacher might go about helping children to achieve objectives she has in mind for them.**

When we were constructing them, we formed working parties of teachers to discuss and try out ideas that we thought might be incorporated in the Units, and to see what happened when children applied their own thinking and their own ways of working to situations we sketched out for them. The information we gathered helped us to produce drafts of the Units; these we tried out informally in other schools and as a result produced, with the aid of our publishers, trial Units to be used in the Pilot Areas scattered throughout the country. Each of the Pilot Areas in England and Wales appointed an Area Representative who administered the trial and evaluation procedures in his area. All Area Representatives met periodically to review the situation and help to make procedures smoother. In Scotland the administration was, naturally enough, somewhat different but broadly on similar lines. This is not the place to describe trials, the process of evaluation and the results produced. We need only say that the evaluation of the pilot trials was aimed at revealing the extent to which the trial Unit helped teachers to consider profitably the objectives for children learning science and to implement them. There is positive evidence that the Units are of value in doing this.

The link between Units

It is a fair question to ask if the Units taken together are intended to form a pattern; are they separate individual studies or are there links between them? The answer is that the Units have not been fitted into a preconceived pattern of subject matter—there is no syllabus, but they are linked, and linked very firmly, by the guide to *Objectives for children learning science* and the philosophy that underlies it. Subject matter was not ignored; the Units were spread as widely as possible among the areas of study likely to be established in schools. How then were the Units chosen, since the field of choice is so wide and so open?

Largely the choice was the personal one of team members, made after considerable discussion, who thought that the subject-area chosen would be one in which they, personally, could point to experiences for children likely to further the attainment of the objectives they had in mind. It soon emerged that a Unit, to be a good one, must have certain attributes:

1. It must be attractive to both children and teachers.

2. The content area must be near to children; that is (*a*) it engages their attention; (*b*) it gives

them opportunity to do something, to construct, to collect, to explore and find out; (c) it stimulates them to think for themselves and causes spontaneous discussion.

3. It must be realisable, given the circumstances of the school. This also means that it can be conducted in a variety of situations.

4. It must lend itself to development; that is, it must suggest interesting possibilities.

5. It must further the teacher's objectives for the children, and be seen to be likely to do so.

6. It must give the kind of help that the teacher needs; not only long-term help, as through pointing out realisable objectives, but short-term help with methods and apparatus.

Making use of the Units

The aim of the Project, as expressed in the terms of reference set out before it began, has been 'to assist teachers to help children, through discovery methods, to gain experience and understanding of the environment and to develop their powers of thinking effectively about it'. This aim has been kept firmly in mind, but of course there is no one way of 'assisting teachers' which would suit all. Teachers' needs for assistance in helping children learn science vary widely according to their background of knowledge in science, their awareness of how children's ideas in science develop, and their own personal interest.

In writing the Units we have tried to make them capable of being used flexibly so that teachers may take from them the help for which they feel a need and be able to find this without being forced to work according to a scheme. This has satisfied many whose comments show sympathy with our problem of finding the right balance, for as one teacher put it, 'More guidance would make the Units too directed or "schemey"; less would

be too sketchy.' But of course it is inevitable that some will not be satisfied, for example, those who would like a course laid out for their children to follow.

Teachers who have tried the Units during their development have used them in a variety of ways. In some cases the pattern has been to follow the suggestions quite closely for one or two Units and then, when both teacher and class are used to working in this way, to use the Units to 'dip into' as sources of suggestions for activities and to refresh their ideas about the purpose and value of the work. In other cases, where children are already learning through discovery methods their teachers would probably agree with the one who wrote that, whatever was already being done in science by the children, it was still 'very stimulating to have available such a fund of ideas'. We do not expect that any teacher would use every part of every Unit, but rather hope that each will choose from what is offered the starting points and ideas for development which suit his or her unique requirements.

Many teachers who have a sound background of science find the Units as helpful as those who have not this background. Few adults today experienced genuine discovery during their early schooling, and the science teaching methods they did experience are not a good pattern to follow when helping young children begin to explore their surroundings with understanding. The kind of assistance the Units can give in these cases is in providing suggestions for leading questions which guide the children towards finding out for themselves, and in emphasising the value of the process of inquiry rather than the importance of learning facts.

The practical consequences of children learning through discovery

Throughout this book and the Project's Units we have tried to exemplify what we mean by a 'discovery approach' to learning. There are several important consequences of working in this way which can have a wide effect on the organisation of work in a classroom and indeed in the school as well. At the risk of repeating what has already been implied, it seems as well to bring out these points explicitly.

'Trying to reproduce a wattle and daub wall. Science or history; does it matter?'

When children are being encouraged to find problems and investigate them as a normal way of learning, they will find problems they want to investigate at all times, not just when 'Science' is on the timetable. It is important for young children to start work on what is intriguing them pretty soon after finding it, so as to take advantage of their motivation for solving the problem. To try to confine problem finding and solving to a certain time each week would be to effectively discourage it, since it must mean that at other times in the week problems would have to be ignored or held over to the prescribed time. This means that a questioning, inquiring approach has to be pursued at any time if it is to be pursued at all. We have, indeed, found that Science 5/13 materials have their greatest effect when a discovery approach is used in all areas of the curriculum and not just in science. **The consequences of this are that activities recognisable as 'science' activities are likely to be pursued at various times and, conversely, that a great deal of 'science'** **may come out of activities not recognisable in the first instance as 'science'.**

It also follows that when children are genuinely encouraged to find problems which interest them then they are most unlikely to choose the same ones. The children in a class have to be treated as individuals not as a single body if 'discovery' work is to be genuine. The children may form into groups for work on common or related problems, but the groups will split up and reform in different combinations as the inquiries and activities of the individuals change. To prevent this choice of working group, by requiring children to keep to groups selected by the teacher, will obviously restrict the freedom of some children to work on problems which really interest them. It is asking a great deal of teachers to follow the progress of each child separately but there is evidence to confirm that this effort is well worth making. **Real discovery work requires that children shall be allowed to work individually or in small groups and not as a whole class.**

Working individually or in small groups

In addition there are considerable practical consequences of discovery work. It will affect the look of the classroom and the role of the teacher. When the children are working in small groups or individually, the guidance they receive comes from dialogue with their teacher. Often the teacher has no more idea of the solution to a problem than the child, but during discussion between them the teacher can help the child to see where his approach to the problem might be at fault, where he might be making false assumptions, where the number of variables in a situation might be greater than he had first thought. But in order to have time for these essential discussions it is necessary for the teacher to arrange things so that the other children in the class can be getting on with their particular work, can find materials when they are needed without asking for them, have access to books, know where to find equipment and know that they must tidy it away after use.

To arrange for these things takes two kinds of organisation, one relating to the physical

A working area is best arranged for greatest interest rather than orderliness

'The guidance they receive comes from dialogue with the teacher'

surroundings and one to the responsibility expected of the children. Not much will be said here about the first of these, since there is already a great deal of useful advice which teachers can get, for example in the Nuffield Junior Science Teacher's Guide 1.* We would stress the importance of arranging as much as possible for tables or desks to be grouped irregularly, to allow maximum floor space for working and moving about, and to allow access to bookshelves, displays, cupboards and drawers. How this is done will obviously depend on individual circumstances. The result may seem untidy, but the criterion to be applied is not how orderly the room looks but whether children can find and use in it what they need. **The physical and organisational setting in the classroom has to be conducive to children taking responsibility for their work.**

* *Published by Collins, 1967.*

Why not work out of doors when you can?

A close up of the classroom on page 20 shows shelves transformed into attractive space for displaying and storing children's more bulky work

6 Children from eleven to thirteen

Have they grown up?

We are devoting this chapter to children aged eleven to thirteen because of the particular problems presented by the wide variety of school organisations for this age range and because of the traditional, but false, assumption that all children of this age are ready for a typically 'secondary' approach to science. There is wide acknowledgement that

'much of the thinking of secondary school pupils in their first and second year has the qualities of childhood thinking' *

and yet in practice they are all too frequently expected to learn and behave in a manner which is at variance with their 'childhood thinking'.

In terms of our Stages of development this means that many, probably the majority, of children in this age range are still at Stage 2, or Stage 1 in some cases. All that is said earlier in this book is, therefore, relevant to teachers of children aged eleven to thirteen and indeed this chapter will not make much sense unless previous chapters have been read.

On page 14 we emphasised that the succession of Stages is important, that Stage 1 is a starting point for children encountering science activities for the first time, whatever their age. Most older children pass rapidly through Stage 1 to Stage 2

* *E. A. Peel,* op cit.

but plenty of concrete experience is essential before they reach Stage 3, where development of abstract thinking is beginning. Older children who have had plenty of concrete experiences in science in their primary school will not necessarily be ready for Stage 3 activities, since the amount of experience and the time needed for consolidation of earlier stages vary widely from one child to another.

We strongly urge teachers of children aged eleven to thirteen to give opportunity for this consolidation and to provide appropriate activity for those without this earlier experience. This could be done by making Stage 1 and 2 activities available in the first instance for all children, and introducing Stage 3 activities as children become able to tackle them. Such an arrangement has been found to work well during pilot trials of our Stage 1 and 2 and Stage 3 Units, as is shown in a typical extract from a teacher working with the *Change* Units: 'At the beginning all began on some selected Stage 2 experiments leading into Stage 3. As time went on about a third of the class continued on to Stage 3 whilst the less able remained mainly on Stage 2.'

We must at once acknowledge that there are serious difficulties in putting this into practice. These difficulties, stemming largely from the organisational setting of many children in this age range, have been revealed several times over by pilot trials of Stage 1, 2 and 3 Units, and we discuss them at length later in this chapter.

First, however, let us examine more closely what we mean by Stage 3.

How do we recognise that a child is at Stage 3?

We have described Stage 3 as the part of development in which children are in transition from 'concrete operational' thought to 'formal operational' thought (page 11). These terms are merely convenient labels for ways of dealing with problems which characterise certain points in the continuous development of children's thought. So if we recall and expand on what these labels mean in terms of observable behaviour in science activities, this will help in recognising when a child is, in some respects, at Stage 3.

There is a danger that in trying to clarify we may over-simplify the situation and imply that a child must be entirely either at one Stage or at another. Experience shows that this is not so; a child may respond in a way which is typical of Stage 3 in regard to some problems, probably ones which are familiar and straightforward, but is very likely, at the same time, to respond to more complex and unfamiliar problems through a wholly 'concrete' approach. We should not think of this as a reversion or failure to progress, since it is simply an example of the uneven development which we have mentioned before (page 14) as being quite usual.

Keeping this reservation in mind, we now look at behaviour which indicates Stage 3 thinking. For this purpose we have picked out behaviour in relation to four aspects we believe are among those central to the development of a scientific approach to problems and to formal thinking:

a. Making a formal hypothesis.

b. Sorting our variables.

c. Drawing conclusions and making generalisations.

d. Thinking about abstract things.

Making a formal hypothesis

A hypothesis, as we have said on page 5, is an assumption which is made tentatively for the purpose of testing whether evidence supports or refutes it. It can be tested logically (by argument) or empirically (by observation or experiment). Frequently hypotheses take the form, if not the actual wording, of an IF–THEN statement.

For example, IF the light does not go on THEN the electricity supply has failed. This is not the only hypothesis which could be proposed in such a situation; the light bulb may have failed, the switch be at fault, or there could be some other reason. The first hypothesis to be proposed and tested is generally the one which knowledge from previous observations suggests is likely to be true. If the electricity supply frequently fails then this would be the thing to test first; if not, then the first hypothesis might be that the bulb has failed.

Another example: IF a weight is moved further away from the fulcrum of a balance THEN more weight must be added on the other side to keep it level. This is a hypothesis which can easily be put to the test, but it is not so simple to formulate the hypothesis in the first place. To do so involves narrowing down the general problem (of equilibrium in the balance in this case) and proposing an answer to a question—how can the balance be kept level when the weight is moved further from the fulcrum?—*before the investigation begins*. This is something a child at the stage of concrete operational thought is generally unlikely to do; he finds things out mainly by 'seeing what happens' rather than by stating possibilities and testing to see which corresponds with reality. He keeps, by and large, to the 'actual' and does not speculate about the 'possible'. He may use an IF–THEN statement to describe what he has found, but this is not a hypothesis since it comes after the observation not before it.

But we must remember that the boundary between stages is ragged; there is no clear-cut division between the point where a child does not make hypotheses and the point where he does so. Some hypotheses will be proposed by children whose thinking is predominantly concrete, most likely in situations where the variables are few and easily defined. Gradually the number of situations in which hypotheses can be proposed will increase as development takes place. Progress from one stage to another is thus indicated by a shift of emphasis from a mode of thinking in which hypothesis making takes a minor part to a mode of thinking in which it takes a major part. We can summarise this behaviour relating to making hypotheses in the following way:

A child at Stage 2:
Makes hypotheses only infrequently and in simple situations. Most of his IF—THEN statements are descriptions or reports of what has been found.

A child at Stage 3:
Is beginning to make hypotheses more frequently, to think about possible solutions before testing them out. His thought is beginning to precede his action.

Sorting out variables

In the treatment of variables the child at Stage 3 shows a systematic approach to problems which is absent at earlier stages. On page 14 we described a situation involving spotting a fault in an electric train circuit in which this development is evident. There are many other problems that show the difference equally well. For example, sorting out the variables which affect the time of swing of a simple pendulum is a problem children at Stage 2 find very difficult unless they have had considerable experience of variables in other situations. They tend to vary two things at the same time and so find it impossible to decide the effect of any one alone. Again, if a child is playing with rods of different lengths and thicknesses to find out how easily they bend, it is likely that he finds bendiness is associated with being long and thin. At Stage 2 the separate effects of length and thickness are unlikely to be dissociated; typically, he might compare the bending of a long thin rod with a shorter, wider one, and say this shows both that longer ones bend more easily than shorter ones, and that thinner ones bend more easily

than thicker ones. He would not realise that the failure to keep either length or thickness constant meant that neither relationship had been shown. These particular variables are especially difficult for the child to dissociate because his experience of everyday objects often indicates that bendiness is associated with being long and thin, in a fishing rod for instance. At Stage 3, however, the child is beginning to be able to visualise possibilities rather than actualities and the approach to problems is less tied to the combinations of variables which have been observed. Now he can separate the variable of length from the variable of width in the rod bending, by showing that a longer rod bends more than a shorter one of the same thickness and that a thinner one bends more than a thicker one of the same length. The fact that fishing rods and other bendy things are often long and thin is not such an obstacle to sorting out the variables, since he can increasingly treat problems in a way which is more detached from real situations.

At Stage 3 the isolation and control of variables can be done through thought and not only through action. Combinations of variables likely to produce a desired result can be hypothesised and put to the test. If this does not produce the expected results, other combinations can be tried until all the possibilities are exhausted. The systematic approach ensures that *all* possibilities are tried, whereas the random approach to variables at Stage 2 is unlikely to cover all the possibilities except by pure chance. Give a child four piles of counters, one pile of green, one of blue, one of yellow and one of red, and set him the problem of making as many different combinations of colours as he can using no more than one counter of any colour in each. Children at all Stages might begin the task in the same way, picking combinations of two or three colours at random. But at some point the child who has reached Stage 3 checks to find out which of the possible combinations he has already found and fills in the gaps by mentally taking the colours two at a time, then three at a time and finally all together. The child at Stage 2 has no system for this checking and continues randomly;

he would be unlikely to produce all the possible combinations. This is a contrived situation but there are many problems which children are likely to come across which depend for their solution on the ability to imagine, even if not actually produce, all the combinations of variables which are possible.

Again we must add the proviso that, though these abilities are developing, they will not be exercised by the children in all situations. There are older children, and indeed adults, who in some circumstances are able to isolate and control variables, but in other circumstances are unable to make, or at least do not make, comparisons which are 'fair' in the sense that the variable in question is the only relevant feature which is different between two articles or situations being compared. *Which?* tests show up the false conclusions we often accept without question, as in the case of enzyme washing-powders for instance. When soiled clothes were washed and soaked overnight in an enzyme washing-powder they were shown to be cleaner than equally dirty clothes washed in ordinary washing-powder in the usual way. But the conclusion that the enzyme washing-powder was therefore more effective than the ordinary powder was invalid, however, since there was an uncontrolled variable—the soaking. When this was eliminated, either by soaking clothes washed in both powders or not soaking either set, then the results were different; under the same conditions the washing-powders were equally effective.

The degree of complexity of the situation must be considered in interpreting the generalisations we are making. A child at Stage 2 may indeed separate variables where they are few and obvious, whilst a child at Stage 3 may fail to do so in a more complex situation. There is also the complication of problems in which variables cannot be isolated or controlled, problems in the realms of psychology, economics or sociology, for instance. In these cases there are not only the variables but the relationships between them to consider. It is likely that the essence of such problems can be better grasped after there has been a thorough appreciation of variables in situations where the variables are easily separated.

To summarise, the behaviour relating to sorting out variables can be described as follows:

A child at Stage 2:
Often finds difficulty in separating the effects of two or more variables. He is not systematic in combining variables except in the simplest situations.

A child at Stage 3:
Is able to separate variables with less difficulty, though he may still be unable to do so in complex situations. He is generally more systematic both in separating and combining variables.

Drawing conclusions and making generalisations

The process of drawing a conclusion involves abstracting a relationship from actual situations of experimental results. A child at Stage 2 can arrive at relationships in the concrete situation in which he is experimenting and is normally content to go no further. He is generally content to describe rather than explain his findings. By contrast, at Stage 3 there is an attempt to put experimental findings into a wider framework, to explain them in terms of relationships which apply more widely than just to the one situation.

The kinds of explanations children give for why some things float in water whilst others sink show the difference well. At Stage 2 the reason for a block of wood floating is that 'the water holds it up'. That 'the water' in question here is the total water in the vessel being used can be gathered from the child's prediction that the same block would sink in a smaller amount of water, since there would not be enough water to hold it up. Another object, such as a key, sinks because 'it is too heavy for the water'. In both cases the explanation is confined to the particular objects and there is no indication of awareness that there might be a relationship which applies to all objects and any amount of water. The two rather different reasons given by the same child for the behaviour of the wood and the key do not worry the child. A child at Stage 3, on the other hand, though he is not able to give a correct explanation, since this involves the fairly advanced concepts of upthrust and displacement, typically shows realisation that the particular sizes of the objects and the amounts of water are immaterial. 'It depends on what it's made of ; wood can be heavy and still float.' 'It depends whether it's lighter or heavier than water.' In this case the 'water' is the water occupying the same volume as the object. 'You take the same amount of water and if it's more [than the weight of the water] the thing sinks but, if it's less the thing floats.' This explanation is independent of what the 'thing' is and can readily be applied in many different situations.

Remembering that these are general remarks which apply in the main, but not without exception, we can summarise behaviour relating to conclusions and generalisations in the following way :

A child at Stage 2:
Is satisfied when he has solved the particular problem and is unlikely to try to abstract from it a principle which might apply in other situations, or to explain it in terms of a generalisation.

A child at Stage 3:
Is more likely to go beyond the solution of a particular problem and to search for an explanation in terms of a general principle. Rather than being content to describe his results, he thinks about them, and may arrive at conclusions by considering abstract relationships as well as concrete situations.

Thinking about abstractions
At Stage 2 a child's mental operations (actions carried out in thought) are mainly concerned with concrete things, which have a real existence for the child. He cannot readily manipulate mentally things which are of a symbolic or abstract nature. Take for instance any version of the not unfamiliar quiz question : If John is taller than Paul and Peter is shorter than Paul who is the tallest, John,

Peter or Paul ? The solution of this would be simple for a very young child if there were real people to compare but in the form in which there are only *statements* to think about the problem is quite difficult. Children at Stage 3 can make an attempt at solving it, but for those at earlier stages the problem is almost impossible unless some concrete representation of the situation is constructed. Stage 3 thinking is beginning to deal with 'what might be' and not just 'what is'. It is being released from the confines of actuality and gradually extending towards encompassing extrapolations far beyond experience, to such ideas as weightlessness, the expansion of the universe, multi dimensional space, and so on.

The development of this ability shows itself in relation to the properties of materials and objects. Gradually a child can entertain the idea of physical properties in isolation from the particular things which have the properties : for example, thinking about 'elasticity' as a subject rather than only about elastic springs, elastic bands, bouncing balls, etc. At Stage 2 such an abstract idea is practically meaningless, for one cannot feel or see 'elasticity'. But for the Stage 3 child it is beginning to have meaning as a useful concept which explains the behaviour of various elastic materials or objects. How soon particular abstract properties can be grasped and thought about will depend on how much concrete experience of things with these properties the child has had, as well as on the degree of abstraction they involve—for example, specific heat will be far more difficult than density, whilst surface tension may be readily grasped if there has been plenty of first-hand exploration, but very obscure without it.

To summarise our comments in relation to thinking about abstractions :

A child at Stage 2:
Can reason logically but is very dependent upon information from his senses. If he has not had direct experience of a situation he is unlikely to be able to reason about it.

A child at Stage 3:

May still prefer to think and deal with concrete material but his gradually developing ability to manipulate mentally shows in an increased power of reasoning.

The four aspects we have discussed are essential to what is generally recognised as adult rational thinking. Their development is extended over several years and very few children in the age range eleven to thirteen will reach Piaget's stage of formal operational thinking. Some children may begin to develop these abilities at this age, a few gifted ones may have begun to do so earlier, and for the less gifted it will be later.

How many at Stage 3 ?

In an article in *Education in Chemistry** the head of science in a large secondary school drew attention to the importance of taking account of children's mental development in planning science work at the secondary stage. Of the concrete operational stage he wrote :

. . . children will be helped considerably in working through it by the activity methods and greater variety of apparatus now in the primary schools.' He continued : 'This is the point where secondary school science and maths teachers must have a clear picture of what is involved. Many of their pupils will still need much work in their first two secondary years merely to consolidate this [Piaget's concrete operational] stage, and even the brightest pupils may need more opportunities to handle weight and measurement and volume operations before they can make much sense of science.'

From his experience of children combined with a knowledge of Piaget's ideas this teacher estimated that only three percent of children at the age of eleven and ten percent at the age of

* Michael Shayer, 'How to assess science courses', Education in Chemistry, *1970, pages 182–6.*

thirteen have reached the stage of formal operations. These figures may only be rough but they do suggest that the proportion of children at our Stage 3, that is in transition from concrete to formal operations, is likely to be smaller than might be supposed. They serve to emphasise our own experience that :

Children between the ages of eleven and thirteen are not all at our Stage 3. At eleven more will be at Stage 2 than Stage 3 ; by thirteen the proportion at Stage 3 will have increased but many will still be at Stage 2, a few even at Stage 1.

It is indeed a challenge to provide suitable learning experience for an age group in which such developmental differences occur.

Stage 3 objectives

The development of the mental abilities which characterise Stage 3 cannot be forced, neither does it seem to be automatic on achieving a certain level of maturity in the brain. The mental manipulations required in abstract and logical thinking do not exist as it were, ready-made, to be slipped into action at the right moment. Instead they have to be built up through a process in which experiences both in and out of school have a large part to play. This process of 'accommodation', or repeated adjustment to the environment has already been mentioned (page 14). Both the physical and social environment are involved ; if the social environment does not encourage this adjustment, as for instance in the case of some primitive societies,* logical thinking as we recognise it is unlikely to develop. If we wish our pupils to develop the power of logical thought we must consciously work towards this end.

*M. Mead, in Discussions in Child Development, *vol. 3, London: Tavistock Publications, 1958, pages 61–2.*

Not only then must there be in the children the potential for progress, but it must be developed if it is to be realised. If we wish to develop the power of thinking we must give children opportunity and encouragement to exercise this power. It can be done through working on problems which are seen by the children as real, interesting and important to them. Vital and thought-provoking work is less likely to follow if the children are bored and frustrated and if the only reason for the activity is that it is on the syllabus.

The Project is trying to help teachers see the point of their work in terms of development of their children's thinking, in helping their children to learn how to learn. So our objectives for Stage 3 are framed in terms of abilities we have discussed above. For example, some of the objectives whose achievement would help develop the power of abstracting the essentials from a problem so as to draw conclusions from it or to generalise are :

3.05 Willingness to examine evidence critically.

3.41 Attempting to identify the essential steps in approaching a problem scientifically.

3.74 Ability to use analogies to explain scientific ideas and theories.

3.91 Ability to draw from observations conclusions that are unbiased by preconception.

3.95 Appreciation of the need to integrate findings into a simplifying generalisation.

3.96 Willingness to check that conclusions are consistent with further evidence.

Some relating to making hypotheses are :

3.06 Willingness to consider beforehand the usefulness of the results from a possible experiment.

3.33 Ability to formulate hypotheses not dependent upon direct observation.

3.34 Ability to extend reasoning beyond the actual to the possible.

3.42 Ability to design experiments with effective controls for testing hypotheses.

Others relate less obviously to one or another of the four abilities discussed in detail ; they may be connected with more than one or with other abilities, such as with applying learning from one situation to a problem in another situation. Applying learning is a manifestation of the ability to think in terms of the possible and the abstract. In searching for clues as to what previous learning might be applicable to a problem, the child who can think in these terms is able to take into account connections through ideas and theories and is not restricted to what is suggested by the physical features of a concrete situation. Objectives which relate to this development are :

3.12 Willingness to extend methods used in science activities to other fields of experience.

3.22 Ability to distinguish observations which are relevant to the solution of a problem from those which are not.

3.63 Ability to apply relevant knowledge without help of contextual cues.

3.86 Appreciation of the social implications of man's changing use of materials, historical and contemporary.

3.87 Appreciation of the social implications of research in science.

3.88 Appreciation of the role of science in the changing pattern of provision for human needs.

Helping children to see the point of their work

At Stage 3 children's growing ability to think logically is used in many different aspects of their lives. Together with the physical and emotional changes which will, for most of them, be beginning at about the same time, this can produce a severely critical attitude to the habits and opinions of their elders and to the things they are asked to do. The problems of adolescents and pre-adolescents are very real and very important to their education, but we cannot go into them here except to mention one result of their reappraisal of previously accepted situations which is particularly relevant. Children at this stage begin to question the purpose of their work at school. It often appears as a negative approach: 'can't see the point of doing this'. In fairness it must be admitted that sometimes this is justified: it is hard to see the point of some introductory exercises in some science courses; happily there are fewer of this kind than there were. But at other times the criticism is a plea for discussion of the work at a new level. The immediate satisfaction of finding out, the achievement of short-term goals, is no longer enough for children whose spheres of thinking are extending. Like their teacher they wish to have a mental picture of where things are leading and it seems not unreasonable that they should know, and have some part in determining, the objectives of their work.

During trials of our Units in secondary schools one sensitive teacher working with first- and second-year pupils reported that he found the children liked to know why they were doing things, and so he discussed the aims of the work with them. The children suggested ways of working towards the aims and they seemed to be on the look-out for things which contributed to these aims. They linked one experience with another in terms of what they were learning from them. The teacher felt that, in time, the children might even suggest the aims themselves.

Science activities and logical thinking

Consistent logical thinking is desirable in many areas of the curriculum and equally in everyday life. As we have said, it does not appear spontaneously; its development depends not only on brain maturation but also on educational experiences which encourage the mental changes as they become potentially possible. The kinds of concrete experience which are necessary precursors to this development can be very adequately provided by the exploration of the physical environment which we call early science. The science which comes later, building on this exploration, is equally well suited to promoting logical, internally consistent thinking. The child-like logic which was developed in Stage 1 and 2 for dealing with concrete objects is, in Stage 3, beginning to be used for dealing with abstract things.

As we have already said, though, we must not assume that because a child is beginning to reason logically in some areas that he will do so in all that he does. We know that this is not so. A child can be at Stage 3 in some respects and still at Stage 2 in others, particularly in new fields of activity.

That a logical or 'scientific' approach to problems is a common aim of several curriculum subject-areas is a strong argument for an integrated approach to learning as far as possible whilst children's development is going on. A logical approach is as important to historical evidence as it is to experimental evidence. The historical and experimental activities could both contribute to and benefit from the development of logical thinking more efficiently if the mode of reasoning is seen to be the same in both cases, and not in effect labelled 'history reasoning' and 'science reasoning'. We say more of this on page 54.

Approach and content

The approach we are advocating for all children in the years eleven to thirteen is the same whether they have reached Stage 3 or not. It is essentially child-centred; that is, we are thinking primarily of *how* we can help children to learn rather than *what* we should teach them. Nevertheless what the children learn is important and we must discuss the basis for choosing the content of their work.

A secondary science teacher discussing the 'problem' of taking first-year children from a variety of primary schools made this point: 'What they *know* when they come is unimportant—they will all have picked up a different collection of facts—but there is only one way of finding out, and if they are able to do this then they will soon get to know the facts which are really important.' Children who have had a chance to 'find out' in their primary classes have a good foundation to work on; others will need to build up this foundation, but all will benefit later in their secondary career from an emphasis on learning to learn rather than on learning facts in their first two secondary years.

Within limits the content of what is found out is not important; the value lies in the process of finding out. But the process cannot exist without some content, the 'something' which is found out. There is an enormous choice of subject, problems and investigations—how does one decide which interests to stimulate, which activities to cater for, in which direction to guide the work?

As at earlier ages interest is a paramount criterion for choice of content. Interest, however, can be stimulated and it is part of a teacher's work to enlarge interests, so this still leaves the field wide open. Two characteristics of this age, however, provide other criteria for choosing the content of the work; interests are sustained much longer than before, and there is a desire to see how one part of the work connects with another. It thus becomes a factor of importance to provide for this preference for continuity and sequence in their work.

In considering content we must, of course, give some thought to how important it is to provide a suitable foundation for the science work that will come after the age of thirteen. The Project team-members do not regard the preparation for work to be done in later years as the most important consideration for deciding content, but it should be taken into account where there are no conflicting or over-riding determinants of content. Our position in this matter can be simply stated: if, as we believe, the process of learning by finding out and the developing of interests, scientific concepts and logical thinking can be encouraged equally well by working in a wide variety of different content areas, then one might as well choose to work in those areas which lay a foundation for later work. Whatever is done in this period will form the foundation for future work in any case. Where there is choice of content, therefore, it is our duty to see that the things which are more important to learn are included.

This point of view and the desirability of catering for more sustained and connected themes in the work led us to frame the Stage 3 objectives which refer to content. These can be found under the broad aims .50/.60 *'Acquiring knowledge and learning skills'*, and .80 *'Appreciating patterns and relationships'*.

Putting principles into practice

A good educational process is so finely balanced and so individual that it is difficult to make an unequivocal statement about it without having to modify the statement so much that its impact is lessened and its value lost. To some degree this applies to what follows, but we will try to preserve its form without losing its reality.

Nobody is better aware than a teacher of the approximate nature of education as it is revealed in the classroom. In spite of manifest difficulties of accommodation, supplies, organisation, training, it goes on with a fair degree of success adjusted to its circumstances through human relations. There is the feeling that if this difficulty or that could be removed the solution to problems would be just around the corner. But would it ? The solution round the corner may be better than the present one but it is still likely only to be partial, a seventy-five per cent solution in which the missing twenty-five per cent contains a higher proportion than before of the things that can be managed without.

The problems of teaching science to pupils between the ages of eleven and thirteen are resolved by such solutions : the situation is inevitably one of compromise, and the better one understands the nature of the compromise the better is one likely to adjust its elements so that the missing twenty-five per cent is reduced and what is left contains a greater proportion of factors that are helpful.

Many people are concerned in this compromise, the Department of Education and Science, the local education authority, the headmaster, the teacher, the parents and not least the children. The Department and the authority would like to provide better accommodation and more facilities, the headmaster would like to resolve conflicting demands of school organisation, the teacher would like to think 'If only . . .' less often ; parents and children the same. Let us look, then, at a few of the elements in this compromise and see, when we do so, what light it throws on a teacher's problems and the solutions that she might choose to adopt. She might be able to say 'For me, this and this are the most important things, and these I can manage to do : that and that are less important and I can't do much about them anyway. I will give most attention then to the things I can do well and which will benefit my pupils most.'

1. She must do her best to understand the natures of the children she is dealing with. We have already said a good deal here that is relevant, and doubtless there is a good deal more that could be said, but nothing replaces her sensitive perception of their needs and the children's assurance of her understanding.

She may have children at Stage 2 and Stage 3 in the same class ; she may even have children at Stage 1. We have tried to give her help in identifying their individual stages of educational development ; she will also have to meet their educational, even their personal, needs.

2. She must have a good idea of what she wants them to achieve through work in science. Here we have suggested guide-lines that she can follow as far as she sees they suit her circumstances, and that she can use to formulate guide-lines of her own.

3. She must know about the materials and processes through which she is going to help her pupils learn. The Units that we have written might give her help from the points of view that we have written them, but there are other projects with different points of view : they might be closer to her own than ours. Perhaps her circumstances are best met by mining several projects to her pupils' best advantage.

4. She must understand the ways in which she could help her pupils learn. There are many forms of teaching, of greater or less directness : most of them are appropriate at some time or other whatever the form of general organisation in the class. She must know the advantages that each can offer, and when they are best employed in her own circumstances.

5. She will know what educational courses are open to her pupils when they leave her, and though she might be unwise to let considerations of the future dominate her conduct of the present, she will certainly wish to make a smooth join between what her pupils are doing now and what they are to do later. In the same way, where she has a free choice of subject-matter through which they are to learn, she might be well advised to choose that which aids the formation of concepts they will need later.

6. She must be able to provide the equipment that her pupils will find essential. Here much depends on the school and the local authority. It is unlikely that they will give her everything she needs, but if she has thought out what she wants,

and has told it to those who regulate the supply, she stands a better chance of getting it than if she keeps quiet and leaves the matter to thought-reading.

Many authorities have used teachers' centres as channels through which to augment class equipment. They do so in different ways and in different contexts, but many a teacher has found her class to benefit from what the teachers' centre has supplied.

At the primary stage, where science equipment is of necessity less specialised than it is later, the tradition has grown for the pupils to bring materials to school for the class to use. They have also grown accustomed to designing and making simple apparatus to further their own investigations. These traditions are good and their practice rarely abused; they may well have a value for children in the age-group we are considering here.

7. She should have suitable accommodation in which to do her work. If her accommodation, even after being rearranged as far as possible, is not suited to the work she would like to do, she has little alternative but to adapt the work to the accommodation she has got. It might be of some value then to consider the kinds of accommodation that are suitable to work at the stages we are discussing, though this is not the place for a dissertation on the details of designing a science room.

At the various primary stages the general classroom fits the needs of science work very well. Nowadays these rooms, with their movable tables, can be used flexibly; many have access to school grounds, some even have access to a shared work-space. There is much to be said for a fixed wall-bench with a sink and tap, and much for the provision of gas with a safety-tap in rooms used by the older pupils. A socket from the electricity mains supply is difficult to dispense with nowadays but its use in connection with science work should be circumspect.* The arrangement of the room is bound to be personal,

but much good advice is given by the Nuffield Junior Science Project:† the same is true of keeping animals.‡ A well-designed service-trolley, providing water, gas and electricity, is often a great help.

As the work in science becomes more complex the accommodation needs to be more specialised, and here we must repeat that this is not the place for discussing science accommodation in detail, nor is this Project the only one that should contribute to such a discussion: the issues are too wide. But we can profitably say a little in general terms about provision that might suit work by children on the lines that this Project suggests.

When the kind of work that pupils do outruns the facilities that the classroom can provide, some form of work-space is needed that is provided with services—gas, water, electricity—and equipped with the tools and apparatus that the work requires. The kind of work-space best suited to meet these conditions depends a good deal on the organisation of the school which houses it. It may be open-plan and be shared with other disciplines than science or it may be a special room, a laboratory, devoted solely to science: it may be purpose-built or adapted.

The open-plan work-space supervised by a teacher with specialist knowledge has much to commend it in a school where group work is firmly established, where pupils are accustomed to working outside the classroom and where teachers other than the class-teacher are freely consulted about work related to their special knowledge. Such rooms are the more useful if

---

* Safety at Schools, *Department of Education and Science Pamphlet 33, HMSO, Chapter 3, especially pages 12–14, 'Electricity'.*
† *Nuffield Junior Science, Teacher's Guide 1, Collins, Chapter 5, 'Problems in classroom organisation'.*
‡ *Nuffield Junior Science, Animals and Plants, Collins.*

they contain bays that groups of pupils can occupy temporarily, and where work in progress can be left in place. In new schools, especially small ones, built to a cost-per-place budget, it is often difficult to provide the range of specialised accommodation that is acceptable; an element of sharing then becomes a necessity if it were not planned as educationally desirable.

When a laboratory is provided it, too, must be designed so that it can be used flexibly. Some excellent designs have been produced recently* with services provided at fixed stations so that work-tables can be moved up to them or else can be rearranged in varied patterns to suit the type of work in progress. The demonstration-bench, no longer in the sole occupancy of the teacher, is designed so that it can form part of these patterns.

Storage is always a problem in schools; very often it becomes stringent where equipment for science is concerned. Whether in classroom, open-plan work-space or laboratory the problem needs to be considered carefully† and provision made so that it can be solved.

Another problem that arises as the complexity of science work increases is that of ancillary help. The point at which this becomes necessary depends on the circumstances of the school: sometimes there is a person whose services can be shared by several departments in the school and who can provide sufficient service of the right kind to suffice. Where there is a laboratory, and where there is much apparatus that must be set out, cleared away and serviced, the help of a technician is hard to dispense with: generally it is uneconomical to do so.

Another form of help that most teachers would find profitable is some measure of secretarial help. The more that teachers design work to suit children's individual needs the more they find they require this help. It should not be impossible to widen the functions of the school office so as to offer teachers the assistance they need.

8. She must be able to work with her pupils in ways that are compatible with their previous experience, with the accommodation and materials available and with the organisation of the school as a whole. So far, our considerations have suggested that group work and individual work are called for at least part of the time. If she and her pupils are unaccustomed to working in this way, the implementation of such modes of class organisation needs to be approached with care, and if radical changes are to be made in the way of working, she might be well advised to make these changes slowly. Where she takes her class for large blocks of time, perhaps for large areas of the curriculum, she could begin by setting one small reliable group to work while the rest of the class continue in ways to which they are accustomed, perhaps working in subject-areas other than science. She may soon be able to judge how quickly she is able to develop the new methods. But without knowing intimately the circumstances of a particular class there is no one way of making changes that can be pointed to as better than all others. As in most matters, nothing replaces her own assessment of these circumstances and her own judgement of what is best to do.

Group work that depends for its success on pupils having blocks of time in which to pursue their investigations is difficult, sometimes impossible, to organise well in schools where different subjects have small weekly time-allowances and are taken by different members of staff at stated intervals on a timetable. One might ask whether such a form of organisation is suited to meet the chief needs of all children in the age range we are considering. Some schools have decided that it is not, and have moved towards a more flexible organisation for these pupils.

Further, at the stages we are concerned with, the boundaries between subject-areas are often ill defined; so, not only is a measure of integration

---

* *Department of Education and Science,* Building Bulletins, *Nos. 35 and 39.*
† *O. M. Stepan,* The Storage of Apparatus, *John Murray, 1967.*

of these areas easier to achieve, if it is desirable to achieve it, but a wide choice is possible of subject-matter related to science through which to help children achieve the objectives in mind.

To take this idea one stage further. If the whole of the curriculum were mapped as to the objectives for children as we have mapped the areas related to science, it would be seen straight away that many of the objectives would be common to several subject-areas. Once this is realised, several courses are open. Firstly, one could consciously approach the same objective through more than one subject-area, make an attack upon it from several directions and so perhaps give children a better chance of attaining it than if they approached it from one direction only. Another way might be to decide that certain subject-areas are better suited for work towards achieving certain objectives than others. For instance, one might decide to resolve the matter of understanding variables through work in science, and to establish an understanding of what makes evidence valid through work in history. If the achievement of objectives is considered more important than the ingestion of information, one might find that working in this way saved a considerable amount of time, as when writing in English one uses the matter from a different subject-area. Finally, one could make one's chief attack on an objective in one subject-area and consciously provide other and more minor approaches in different areas. With considerations like these in mind the study of science could be pursued with different intensities at different times.

9. Finally the teacher is almost certain to ask herself at some time if her knowledge of science is sufficient for the work she wants to do. If the children are at Stages 1 and 2 it is unlikely that she will be unable to meet their demands, particularly if she is willing to do the supplementary reading that all teachers need to do at some time in some subject-area. She may be wise to seek the support of other teachers, colleagues at school or at the teachers' centre. The more she can see of what others do the greater confidence she is likely to develop. Where Stage 3 is concerned she

would without doubt benefit from having studied science at main subject level at college, or from having gained more knowledge of the structure of science in some other way. She would certainly need to have done so if she is in the position of having to advise others or to help organise the subject in the school.

When the attempt is made to suit the way of working to children's past experience and their present opportunities the matter of organisation does two things: it both raises problems and conceals them. In his primary school a child may be accustomed to working in most subject-areas with one teacher for large blocks of time; this may be varied by swapping teachers for some activities and, in recent years in some schools, by a certain amount of team-teaching. In his secondary school the offering well might be a subject-oriented timetable taught on a common front to thirty at a time by specialist teachers. To transfer from a child-centred milieu to a subject-centred one is bound to raise difficulties for some children. These difficulties are heightened if in the primary school children are considered to be at the concrete operational stage, and in the secondary school to be well able to make abstractions. So, not only could the change in organisation cause disturbance to the child, but the whole process is bedevilled if he has not made the change expected of him in his way of thinking. He may still be chiefly a concrete operator and may continue to be one for a few years yet. His more developed brother may have been able to work with abstractions while still at the primary school; if so the change might suit him well. But whatever the case may be there is no substitute for recognising the stages of educational development that individual children have reached and then adapting the work they do to suit them.

This brings us back full circle to the considerations with which we began, those of deciding what kind of science is right for the children we work with and what we want them to achieve through the work they do. The decisions we make will come when we look at our work critically, and the purpose of this book is to help us do so.

Appendix

mainly with tensions and compressions in springs, and tensions in the surface of liquids.

Change, Stages 1 & 2 and Background
We accept without question that things often change. This book suggests that children might look critically at some of the changes within their experience.

Change, Stage 3
Change, Stages 1 & 2, dealt with obvious changes; *Change, Stage 3*, explores those less obvious. All change involves energy, and in this book energy changes and chemical changes are linked to children's environments.

Minibeasts, Stages 1 & 2
Worms, slugs, snails, spiders and many kinds of insects are the 'minibeasts' of this Unit. They are introduced from a child's point of view and the book is organised to help teachers develop work arising from children's initial contact with the animals. It gives practical guidance about collecting and keeping minibeasts, and offers numerous suggestions for activities and investigations.

Holes, gaps and cavities, Stages 1 & 2
Young children acquire knowledge, skills and methods of learning in a seemingly haphazard way. This very wide-based title takes advantage of the 'butterflying' nature of children and covers diverse activities ranging from looking for holes in the environment to making sorting machines based on holes and examining the effects of passing liquids through holes.

Trees, Stages 1 & 2
This Unit looks at trees in playgrounds, city streets, town parks and in the countryside. It offers teachers help in appreciating the wide range of activities that can occur when children explore trees. In particular it gives guidance for developing investigations from seasonal observations and collections.

Coloured things, Stages 1 & 2
This Unit includes people, paints, flowers, fabrics, fires and road signs. It is deliberately diverse in subject matter, and gives guidance about activities that can arise from children's natural contact with the colourful things of their environment.

Metals, Stages 1 & 2
Metals are important in our environment and, being so common and so commonplace, are apt to be overlooked by children. This book suggests ways in which children might explore the world of metals and get to know something of their properties.

Metals, Background information
Intended to help teachers by providing them with background knowledge to the investigations suggested in *Metals, Stages 1 & 2*.

Ourselves, Stages 1 & 2
Children are always interested in themselves. The emphasis of this Unit is on aspects of ourselves that can be discovered at first-hand. The activities suggested range from finger-printing and looking at footprints to measuring range of vision and reaction times.

Like and unlike, Stages 1, 2 & 3
In many Units simple observations of the properties of things led to sorting and separating activities. Here, more ideas are collected together and, for those children who have reached Stage 3, these ideas are refined with an eye to some basic notions in science.

Science, models and toys, Stage 3
Intended to carry on the work begun in *Science from toys, Stages 1 & 2*. Ways are suggested for bridging the gap between the methods of primary and secondary schools.

Children and plastics, Stages 1 & 2 and Background
For children, work with plastics could complement that with wood and metals. The objectives are similar and could be achieved by working with this modern material, looking at it and thinking about it critically. The parts intended to provide

background knowledge for the teacher also contain notes on practical work.

Using the environment by Margaret Collis

This series of books is about field studies; they deal with investigations and problems that children can discover and use as a basis for learning when their natural interest in their outdoor surroundings is encouraged. Through the help of many teachers it has been possible to relate them closely to the gradual intellectual development of children and therefore to their changing needs.

Volume 1: *Early explorations*

This is concerned with the earliest work beyond the classroom when children need experience designed to sharpen sensory perception, extend vocabulary and help them to think about the numerical and spatial aspects of their surroundings. Such children will usually be very young but older children, dealing with field work for the first time, will also need some practice in early stages of the work before they become interested in studies appropriate to more experienced investigations.

Volume 2: *Investigations*

This book contains many questions and suggestions designed to help children work actively and purposefully on studies in depth concerned with living things, common materials and everyday situations. They become ready to do this when they find something of particular interest on which they wish to focus attention.

Volume 3: *Tackling problems*

The material in this book could serve as an impetus to children's early investigation of some major biological ideas and relationships through the design of controlled experiments. They will be able to deal with the reasoning this demands as their capacity for abstract thinking develops.

Volume 4: *Ways and means*

Information in this book is relevant to field studies at all times, for it deals with ways and means of providing the facilities, equipment and raw materials children need for a wide range of outdoor investigations and for the activities which result when they return to school.

Objectives for children learning science

Guide lines to keep in mind

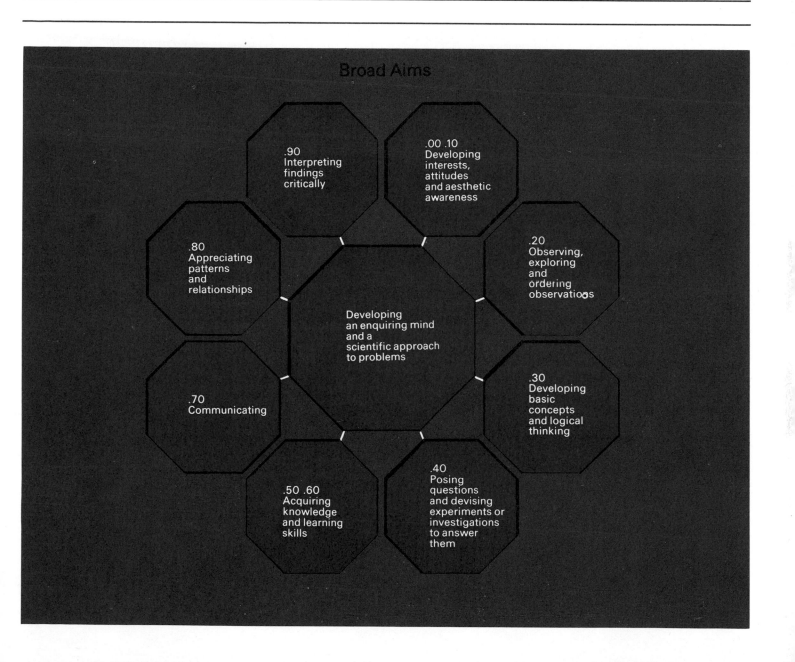

Broad Aims

.90 Interpreting findings critically

.00 .10 Developing interests, attitudes and aesthetic awareness

.80 Appreciating patterns and relationships

.20 Observing, exploring and ordering observations

Developing an enquiring mind and a scientific approach to problems

.70 Communicating

.30 Developing basic concepts and logical thinking

.50 .60 Acquiring knowledge and learning skills

.40 Posing questions and devising experiments or investigations to answer them

What we mean by Stage 1, Stage 2 and Stage 3

Attitudes, interests and aesthetic awareness

.00/.10

Stage 1
Transition from intuition to concrete operations. Infants generally.

The characteristics of thought among infant children differ in important respects from those of children over the age of about seven years. Infant thought has been described as 'intuitive' by Piaget; it is closely associated with physical action and is dominated by immediate observation. Generally, the infant is not able to think about or imagine the consequences of an action unless he has actually carried it out, nor is he yet likely to draw logical conclusions from his experiences. At this early stage the objectives are those concerned with active exploration of the immediate environment and the development of ability to discuss and communicate effectively: they relate to the kind of activities that are appropriate to these very young children, and which form an introduction to ways of exploring and of ordering observations.

1.01 Willingness to ask questions
1.02 Willingness to handle both living and non-living material.
1.03 Sensitivity to the need for giving proper care to living things.
1.04 Enjoyment in using all the senses for exploring and discriminating.
1.05 Willingness to collect material for observation or investigation.

Concrete operations. Early stage.

In this Stage, children are developing the ability to manipulate things mentally. At first this ability is limited to objects and materials that can be manipulated concretely, and even then only in a restricted way. The objectives here are concerned with developing these mental operations through exploration of concrete objects and materials—that is to say, objects and materials which, as physical things, have meaning for the child. Since older children, and even adults, prefer an introduction to new ideas and problems through concrete example and physical exploration, these objectives are suitable for all children, whatever their age, who are being introduced to certain science activities for the first time.

1.06 Desire to find out things for oneself.
1.07 Willing participation in group work.
1.08 Willing compliance with safety regulations in handling tools and equipment.
1.09 Appreciation of the need to learn the meaning of new words and to use them correctly.

Stage 2
Concrete operations. Later stage.

In this Stage, a continuation of what Piaget calls the stage of concrete operations, the mental manipulations are becoming more varied and powerful. The developing ability to handle variables—for example, in dealing with multiple classification—means that problems can be solved in more ordered and quantitative ways than was previously possible. The objectives begin to be more specific to the exploration of the scientific aspects of the environment rather than to general experience, as previously. These objectives are developments of those of Stage 1 and depend on them for a foundation. They are those thought of as being appropriate for all children who have progressed from Stage 1 and not merely for nine- to eleven-year-olds.

2.01 Willingness to co-operate with others in science activities.
2.02 Willingness to observe objectively.
2.03 Appreciation of the reasons for safety regulations.
2.04 Enjoyment in examining ambiguity in the use of words.
2.05 Interest in choosing suitable means of expressing results and observations.
2.06 Willingness to assume responsibility for the proper care of living things.
2.07 Willingness to examine critically the results of their own and others' work.
2.08 Preference for putting ideas to test before accepting or rejecting them.
2.09 Appreciation that approximate methods of comparison may be more appropriate than careful measurements.

Stage 3
Transition to stage of abstract thinking.

This is the Stage in which, for some children, the ability to think about abstractions is developing. When this development is complete their thought is capable of dealing with the possible and hypothetical, and is not tied to the concrete and to the here and now. It may take place between eleven and thirteen for some able children, for some children it may happen later, and for others it may never occur. The objectives of this stage are ones which involve development of ability to use hypothetical reasoning and to separate and combine variables in a systematic way. They are appropriate to those who have achieved most of the Stage 2 objectives and who now show signs of ability to manipulate mentally ideas and propositions.

3.01 Acceptance of responsibility for their own and others' safety in experiments.
3.02 Preference for using words correctly.
3.03 Commitment to the idea of physical cause and effect.
3.04 Recognition of the need to standardise measurements.
3.05 Willingness to examine evidence critically.
3.06 Willingness to consider beforehand the usefulness of the results from a possible experiment.
3.07 Preference for choosing the most appropriate means of expressing results or observations.
3.08 Recognition of the need to acquire new skills.
3.09 Willingness to consider the role of science in everyday life.

Attitudes, interests and aesthetic awareness
.00/.10

Observing, exploring and ordering observations
.20

1.21 Appreciation of the variety of living things and materials in the environment.
1.22 Awareness of changes which take place as time passes.
1.23 Recognition of common shapes—square, circle, triangle.
1.24 Recognition of regularity in patterns.
1.25 Ability to group things consistently according to chosen or given criteria.

1.11 Awareness that there are various ways of testing out ideas and making observations.
1.12 Interest in comparing and classifying living or non-living things.
1.13 Enjoyment in comparing measurements with estimates.
1.14 Awareness that there are various ways of expressing results and observations.
1.15 Willingness to wait and to keep records in order to observe change in things.
1.16 Enjoyment in exploring the variety of living things in the environment.
1.17 Interest in discussing and comparing the aesthetic qualities of materials.

1.26 Awareness of the structure and form of living things.
1.27 Awareness of change of living things and non-living materials.
1.28 Recognition of the action of force
1.29 Ability to group living and non-living things by observable attributes.
1.29a Ability to distinguish regularity in events and motion.

2.11 Enjoyment in developing methods for solving problems or testing ideas.
2.12 Appreciation of the part that aesthetic qualities of materials play in determining their use.
2.13 Interest in the way discoveries were made in the past.

2.21 Awareness of internal structure in living and non-living things.
2.22 Ability to construct and use keys for identification.
2.23 Recognition of similar and congruent shapes.
2.24 Awareness of symmetry in shapes and structures.
2.25 Ability to classify living things and non-living materials in different ways.
2.26 Ability to visualise objects from different angles and the shape of cross-sections.

3.11 Appreciation of the main principles in the care of living things.
3.12 Willingness to extend methods used in science activities to other fields of experience.

3.21 Appreciation that classification criteria are arbitrary.
3.22 Ability to distinguish observations which are relevant to the solution of a problem from those which are not.
3.23 Ability to estimate the order of magnitude of physical quantities.

	Developing basic concepts and logical thinking .30	**Posing questions and devising experiments or investigations to answer them** .40
Stage 1 Transition from intuition to concrete operations. Infants generally.	1.31 Awareness of the meaning of words which describe various types of quantity. 1.32 Appreciation that things which are different may have features in common.	1.41 Ability to find answers to simple problems by investigation. 1.42 Ability to make comparisons in terms of one property or variable.
Concrete operations. Early stage.	1.33 Ability to predict the effect of certain changes through observation of similar changes. 1.34 Formation of the notions of the horizontal and the vertical. 1.35 Development of concepts of conservation of length and substance. 1.36 Awareness of the meaning of speed and of its relation to distance covered.	1.43 Appreciation of the need for measurement. 1.44 Awareness that more than one variable may be involved in a particular change.
Stage 2 Concrete operations. Later stage.	2.31 Appreciation of measurement as division into regular parts and repeated comparison with a unit. 2.32 Appreciation that comparisons can be made indirectly by use of an intermediary. 2.33 Development of concepts of conservation of weight, area and volume. 2.34 Appreciation of weight as a downward force. 2.35 Understanding of the speed, time, distance relation.	2.41 Ability to frame questions likely to be answered through investigations. 2.42 Ability to investigate variables and to discover effective ones. 2.43 Appreciation of the need to control variables and use controls in investigations. 2.44 Ability to choose and use either arbitrary or standard units of measurement as appropriate. 2.45 Ability to select a suitable degree of approximation and work to it. 2.46 Ability to use representational models for investigating problems or relationships.
Stage 3 Transition to stage of abstract thinking.	3.31 Familiarity with relationships involving velocity, distance, time, acceleration. 3.32 Ability to separate, exclude or combine variables in approaching problems. 3.33 Ability to formulate hypotheses not dependent upon direct observation. 3.34 Ability to extend reasoning beyond the actual to the possible. 3.35 Ability to distinguish a logically sound proof from others less sound.	3.41 Attempting to identify the essential steps in approaching a problem scientifically. 3.42 Ability to design experiments with effective controls for testing hypotheses. 3.43 Ability to visualise a hypothetical situation as a useful simplification of actual observations. 3.44 Ability to construct scale models for investigation and to appreciate implications of changing the scale.

1.51 Ability to discriminate between different materials.
1.52 Awareness of the characteristics of living things.
1.53 Awareness of properties which materials can have.
1.54 Ability to use displayed reference material for identifying living and non-living things.

1.55 Familiarity with sources of sound.
1.56 Awareness of sources of heat, light and electricity.
1.57 Knowledge that change can be produced in common substances.
1.58 Appreciation that ability to move or cause movement requires energy.
1.59 Knowledge of differences in properties between and within common groups of materials.

1.61 Appreciation of man's use of other living things and their products.
1.62 Awareness that man's way of life has changed through the ages.
1.63 Skill in manipulating tools and materials.
1.64 Development of techniques for handling living things correctly.
1.65 Ability to use books for supplementing ideas or information.

2.51 Knowledge of conditions which promote changes in living things and non-living materials.
2.52 Familiarity with a wide range of forces and of ways in which they can be changed.
2.53 Knowledge of sources and simple properties of common forms of energy.
2.54 Knowledge of the origins of common materials.
2.55 Awareness of some discoveries and inventions by famous scientists.
2.56 Knowledge of ways to investigate and measure properties of living things and non-living materials.
2.57 Awareness of changes in the design of measuring instruments and tools during man's history.
2.58 Skill in devising and constructing simple apparatus.
2.59 Ability to select relevant information from books or other reference material.

3.51 Knowledge that chemical change results from interaction.
3.52 Knowledge that energy can be stored and converted in various ways.
3.53 Awareness of the universal nature of gravity.
3.54 Knowledge of the main constituents and variations in the composition of soil and of the earth.
3.55 Knowledge that properties of matter can be explained by reference to its particulate nature.
3.56 Knowledge of certain properties of heat, light, sound, electrical, mechanical and chemical energy.
3.57 Knowledge of a wide range of living organisms.
3.58 Development of the concept of an internal environment.
3.59 Knowledge of the nature and variations in basic life processes.

3.61 Appreciation of levels of organisation in living things.
3.62 Appreciation of the significance of the work and ideas of some famous scientists.
3.63 Ability to apply relevant knowledge without help of contextual cues.
3.64 Ability to use scientific equipment and instruments for extending the range of human senses.

Communicating	Appreciating patterns and relationships
.70	.80

Stage 1
Transition from
intuition to
concrete
operations.
Infants
generally.

1.71 Ability to use new words appropriately.
1.72 Ability to record events in their sequences.
1.73 Ability to discuss and record impressions of living and non-living things in the environment.
1.74 Ability to use representational symbols for recording information on charts or block graphs.

1.81 Awareness of cause-effect relationships.

- -

Concrete
operations.
Early stage.

1.75 Ability to tabulate information and use tables.
1.76 Familiarity with names of living things and non-living materials.
1.77 Ability to record impressions by making models, painting or drawing.

1.82 Development of a concept of environment.
1.83 Formation of a broad idea of variation in living things.
1.84 Awareness of seasonal changes in living things.
1.85 Awareness of differences in physical conditions between different parts of the Earth.

Stage 2
Concrete
operations.
Later stage.

2.71 Ability to use non-representational symbols in plans, charts, etc.
2.72 Ability to interpret observations in terms of trends and rates of change.
2.73 Ability to use histograms and other simple graphical forms for communicating data.
2.74 Ability to construct models as a means of recording observations.

2.81 Awareness of sequences of change in natural phenomena.
2.82 Awareness of structure-function relationship in parts of living things.
2.83 Appreciation of interdependence among living things.
2.84 Awareness of the impact of man's activities on other living things.
2.85 Awareness of the changes in the physical environment brought about by man's activity.
2.86 Appreciation of the relationships of parts and wholes.

Stage 3
Transition to
stage of
abstract
thinking.

3.71 Ability to select the graphical form most appropriate to the information being recorded.
3.72 Ability to use three-dimensional models or graphs for recording results.
3.73 Ability to deduce information from graphs : from gradient, area, intercept.
3.74 Ability to use analogies to explain scientific ideas and theories.

3.81 Recognition that the ratio of volume to surface area is significant.
3.82 Appreciation of the scale of the universe.
3.83 Understanding of the nature and significance of changes in living and non-living things.
3.84 Recognition that energy has many forms and is conserved when it is changed from one form to another.
3.85 Recognition of man's impact on living things— conservation, change, control.
3.86 Appreciation of the social implications of man's changing use of materials, historical and contemporary.
3.87 Appreciation of the social implications of research in science.
3.88 Appreciation of the role of science in the changing pattern of provision for human needs.

Interpreting findings critically

.90

1.91 Awareness that the apparent size, shape and relationships of things depend on the position of the observer.

- -

1.92 Appreciation that properties of materials influence their use.

2.91 Appreciation of adaptation to environment.
2.92 Appreciation of how the form and structure of materials relate to their function and properties.
2.93 Awareness that many factors need to be considered when choosing a material for a particular use.
2.94 Recognition of the role of chance in making measurements and experiments.

3.91 Ability to draw from observations conclusions that are unbiased by preconception.
3.92 Willingness to accept factual evidence despite perceptual contradictions.
3.93 Awareness that the degree of accuracy of measurements has to be taken into account when results are interpreted.
3.94 Awareness that unstated assumptions can affect conclusions drawn from argument or experimental results.
3.95 Appreciation of the need to integrate findings into a simplifying generalisation.
3.96 Willingness to check that conclusions are consistent with further evidence.

These Stages we have chosen conform to modern ideas about children's learning. They conveniently describe for us the mental development of children between the ages of five and thirteen years, but it must be remembered that ALTHOUGH CHILDREN GO THROUGH THESE STAGES IN THE SAME ORDER THEY DO NOT GO THROUGH THEM AT THE SAME RATES.
SOME children achieve the later Stages at an early age.
SOME loiter in the early Stages for quite a time.
SOME never have the mental ability to develop to the later Stages.
ALL appear to be ragged in their movement from one Stage to another.
Our Stages, then, are not tied to chronological age, so in any one class of children there will be, almost certainly, some children at differing Stages of mental development.